RESEARCH WORKS

Papers from the AMSO Research
Effectiveness Awards, 1991

Association of Market Survey Organisations

Edited and introduced by
Derek Martin
and
John Goodyear

NTC PUBLICATIONS LIMITED

First published 1992 by **NTC Publications Limited**
Farm Road, Henley-on-Thames, Oxfordshire, RG9 1EJ, United Kingdom
Telephone: 0491 574671

Copyright © NTC Publications Limited 1992

All rights reserved. No part of this publication may be reproduced or transmitted in any form or by any means, electronic or mechanical including photocopying, recording or any information storage or retrieval system, without prior permission in writing from the publishers.

British Library Cataloguing in Publication Data
Research Works.
  I. Association of Market Survey Organisations
  658.83

ISBN 1-870562-96-8

Typeset in 11/13 pt Times by NTC Publications Ltd
Printed and bound in Great Britain by
Biddles Ltd, Guildford and King's Lynn

CONTENTS

AMSO Research Effectiveness Awards 1991 — v

CHAPTER 1	**THE SAMARITANS** Reaching Out With Research		1
First Prize	Nicky Buss Mike Leibling Michelle Jacobs Ricky Wright	Saatchi & Saatchi Saatchi & Saatchi Audience Selection National Opinion Polls	
CHAPTER 2	**FROM PILLAR-BOX TO DOOR MAT** Royal Mail's 'End-To-End' Survey and Its Impact on The Bottom Line		23
Second Prize	Diana Brown Roger Banks Sheila Jones	Royal Mail Research International Research International	
CHAPTER 3	**TOWARDS MORE EFFECTIVE PROMOTIONS**		33
Third Prize	Ian Fryer Marc Drake	Heinz Taylor Nelson	
CHAPTER 4	**TOWARDS AN ACTION PLAN** Acting on the Results of a Tenants' Survey		47
Highly Commended	Derrick Dyas Tim Burns	Warwick District Council MORI	

Contents iv

CHAPTER 5	**HOW RESEARCH HELPED THAMES TELEVISION DEVELOP ITS STRENGTHS IN EFFECTIVELY RESEARCHING THE BUSINESS COMMUNITY**		63

Highly Commended David Harrison   Thames Television
              Neil Eddleston   Thames Television
              John Bermingham BMRB

CHAPTER 6	**PROFESSIONAL SERVICES IN AGRICULTURE** The Market for Commercial and 'Public Good' Advice		86

Commended   John Lockhart   BJM Research & Consultancy

CHAPTER 7	**FROM DOLL'S HOUSE TO DYING** Alarmingly Effective Research		102

Commended   Ian Brace   BJM Research & Consultancy

CHAPTER 8	**HOW TARGET GROUP RATINGS ALLOWED TV-am TO MAKE THEIR CLIENTS AN OFFER THEY COULD NOT REFUSE**		118

Commended   David Bergg   TV-am
              Jim Kite   TV-am
              Richard Silman BMRB

CHAPTER 9	**IT DOES MORE THAN YOU'D CREDIT**		138

Commended   John McGill   Barclaycard
              Vicki Drummond   A.C. Nielsen

Index   155

AMSO
RESEARCH EFFECTIVENESS AWARDS
1991

INTRODUCTION

The AMSO Research Effectiveness Awards scheme is designed to be a major competition for papers demonstrating the practical value of research in guiding and improving business or policy decision-making, and thereby – directly or indirectly – resulting in improvements in the user's business.

It is the market research industry's counterpart to the successful IPA Advertising Effectiveness Awards scheme; it is a biennial Awards scheme, and operates in alternate years to the IPA competition.

BACKGROUND

AMSO – the Association of Market Survey Organisations – is the UK's major trade association for the research industry. It was established in the mid-1960's and has grown to the point where its member companies account for some two-thirds of all commercially available research in the UK – as well as carrying out and co-ordinating a significant amount of international research.

AMSO's objectives as an organisation are reproduced in full later in this book, but the decision to initiate, fund and operate the Research Effectiveness Awards scheme arises from – and is in support of – three of those objectives, namely:

- stimulating demand for, and promoting the value of, market, marketing, social and opinion research and research-based consultancy, domestically and internationally.

- promoting high quality standards in market research generally, and upholding those high standards amongst AMSO members in particular.

- providing existing and potential clients with encouragement, reassurance, support and justification for their selection of an AMSO member supplier in preference to a non-member.

OBJECTIVES

The specific objectives of the AMSO Research Effectiveness Awards scheme, then, are :

1. To demonstrate the practical value of research to management in guiding and improving decision-making, illustrating this through case histories of business success where research can be cited as a major relevant factor.

2. To show, by detailed analysis of the business issues and the research undertaken, how research can improve the quality of decision-making, and to demonstrate the professional skills and standards of the British research industry.

3. To provide clear evidence of the value of research through its pay-off in improved sales and profitability – but also in its contribution to other aspects of the client's business, such as cost control, distribution, staff effectiveness and satisfaction, promotional spend, and any other areas of direct benefit.

4. To help enhance the general understanding of the contribution that research can make to the interpretation and resolution of business and social issues.

It was with these objectives in mind that AMSO launched the Awards scheme in the late Autumn of 1990 for papers to be submitted and evaluated, and prizes and commendations awarded, in 1991.

THE AWARDS SCHEME : INVITATION AND EVALUATION

The invitation to enter papers for the AMSO awards self-evidently sought papers which would demonstrate 'research effectiveness', but the range of subject matter from which such papers could be drawn was deliberately broad.

AMSO was looking for papers which, overall, would demonstrate the true diversity of the research function and contribution, ranging from data collection, through to such areas as consultancy, modelling or strategy analysis.

There was no requirement for papers to be limited to 'conventional' research studies involving a stated problem, research design, original data collection, analysis and interpretation: papers could also be about designing and carrying out experiments, re-analysing existing data, modelling or forecasting.

The only proviso being that the research itself – or as a minimum the data collection – must have been carried out by an AMSO member company.

Team entries – research agency plus client – were encouraged, and written permission from the client or the owner of the research to publish the case study details was mandatory before the paper was accepted by the judges.

Copyright in the papers submitted for the Research Effectiveness Awards is ceded to AMSO.

In evaluating the papers received according to a consistent set of parameters, the judges gave due weight to such factors as the quality of the research, its design, the methods of data collection and the perceived and demonstrated results – but the critical criteria in judging remained the extent to which the research as presented made an effective/demonstrable contribution to an improvement in the client's business success.

CONCLUSIONS

The nine papers which are reproduced in the main section of this book are the first, second and third prize winners, the two papers which were highly commended, and the four papers which were commended by the panel of judges.

Selected by the judging panel from a total of twenty papers entered for this, the first AMSO Research Effectiveness Awards competition, the nine papers selected provide clear evidence of the very wide range of applications for market research.

Clients include commercial television franchisees, government departments, services and advisory services, local government, a charitable organisation, a banking/credit card service and a fast-moving consumer goods company.

The papers which follow show how research has been used, variously, to reduce risk and save money for a major credit card company; to help a government advisory service successfully launch new services and reposition existing ones; to demonstrate the effectiveness of television advertising in reaching the business community; to monitor and, importantly, to improve the Royal Mail's quality of service; to save lives by increasing awareness of the importance of smoke alarms amongst key sectors of the consumer market; to monitor, evaluate and help to improve the effectiveness of Heinz's on-pack promotional activity; etc., etc.

Each paper provides clear evidence of the contribution that research can, and does, make – and the very diversity of applications acts as testimony to the value of research in all areas of business and social activity.

The Council and Members of AMSO are justifiably pleased with the outcome of this first AMSO Research Effectiveness Awards Competition – and would like to thank everyone involved:

- the authors who submitted papers.

- the clients who gave approval for data and results to be published.

- AMSO members who supported the scheme financially through their subscriptions and through their attendance at the subsequent Awards Dinner and Conference.

- members of the IPA and its secretariat – and particularly Janet Mayhew – for their support and advice.

- members of the Judging Panel – and in particular the external/ non-AMSO members of the Judging Panel, all extremely senior individuals representing, variously, management and marketing (Guy Walker), advertising and planning (John Bartle) and business academia (Prof. Michael Thomas).

We are in their debt.

In conclusion, we trust and believe that – just as the IPA's award scheme has grown in size, in sophistication, in status and in importance over the years since it was launched in 1980 – the AMSO Research Effectiveness Awards will enjoy growing success and acclaim in the coming years and will provide ever more effective proof of the very real contribution that well-planned research can make to business success and improved decision-making ... proof that 'Research Works'!

John Goodyear & Derek Martin

AMSO: STATEMENT OF OBJECTIVES

AMSO – the Association of Market Survey Organisations – exists to serve, and to further the best interests of, its member companies, externally and internally, by:

- stimulating demand for, and promoting the value of, market, marketing, social and opinion research and research-based consultancy, domestically and internationally.
- promoting high quality standards in market research generally and upholding those high standards amongst AMSO members in particular.
- providing existing and potential clients with encouragement, reassurance, support and justification for their selection of an AMSO-member supplier in preference to a non-member.
- promoting AMSO as the premier trade association of the research industry and as the resource of first choice for information and informed comment on research- related matters
- providing a forum for discussion of, and a means of communication for, matters of interest to the membership
- providing members with reliable industry informationand statistics to assist their business-planning and management decision-making
- representing the best interests of members through liaison with other relevant bodies and in relation to external influences and pressures.

THE JUDGING PANEL

John Goodyear (Chairman)
    Chairman & Chief Executive: The MBL Group Plc
John Bartle   Joint Chief Executive: Bartle Bogle Hegarty
Bill Blyth   Director: AGB Research
Derek Martin (Awards Secretary)
    Chairman & M.D.: Martin Hamblin Research
Professor Michael Thomas
    Head of Marketing Department: University of Strathclyde
Guy Walker   Chairman: Van den Berghs and Jurgens

1

THE SAMARITANS

REACHING OUT WITH RESEARCH

SUMMARY

Introduction and Business Background

The Samaritans is a charity founded in 1953 to offer sympathetic, caring and confidential support at any time to anyone feeling suicidal or despairing. It has 186 branches nationwide staffed by over 22,000 volunteers, receiving over two and a half million calls for help every year.

Fundraising

In 1989 the financial position of The Samaritans was relatively poor; as a charity, it relied on voluntary funds from the public, but in terms of donations it was relatively insignificant, and seemed to have unusual difficulty raising funds. The Samaritans was concerned to find out how to increase fundraising effectively; it suspected that people might not think of it as a *charity*, and realise that it was dependent on voluntary donations. If this were the case it would obviously be necessary to change the public's perceptions first; large-scale fundraising activity on its own would not be particularly effective.

Positioning

The positioning of The Samaritans' service was also in need of clarification; was it seen as there for the suicidal, the pre-suicidal, or more widely, just as 'someone to talk to'? Historic communication had varied, and there was confusion as to where along this spectrum it lay by its own branches, let alone by the general public and its callers. The Samaritans needed to understand where the public's perceptions lay, to understand where and how changes were needed.

Targeting

The Samaritans was also aware that suicide rates were higher among certain sectors of the population, such as the young and the elderly, but at the time did not specifically target these groups. There was a growing recognition within the charity that its resources might not be targeted most effectively, but before making any decisions, it need to know how far people in these groups were aware of The Samaritans and its services, as the consequences, in terms of re-direction of funds, management structure and promotional activities could be far-reaching for the organisation.

Changes to any of these three areas would potentially have an enormous impact on The Samaritans' financial position and its planned strategy for the movement. Obviously a fair and accurate understanding of the issues and the beliefs and attitudes of the public was essential to test its hypotheses and to provide a sound base for such decisions. The Samaritans believed that such understanding could only come from carefully conducted research.

The Research

The Samaritans commissioned two research studies, conducted in November 1989 by Audience Selection Ltd and NOP Market Research Ltd, with the questionnaire design and analysis specifications advised by Saatchi & Saatchi Advertising Ltd.

The Audience Selection study was a telephone omnibus study of 1,023 adults aged 15+ designed to test people's awareness of The Samaritans *as a charity*, and hence of its needs for funds.

The study by NOP questioned people's awareness and understanding of The Samaritans, and was analysed to evaluate differences between sub-groups. A representative sample of 1,966 adults were interviewed in their homes.

Key Findings and Implications

1) Awareness of The Samaritans as a charity, needing public financial support, was surprisingly low – only 1.36% of respondents mentioned The Samaritans as a *charity* they could think of, and less than half the population realised The Samaritans relies mainly on public funds.

Research had isolated the specific problem; the need was not simply for increased fundraising activities, but for a programme of awareness of The Samaritans and its need for money in conjunction with concentrated targeting of fundraising.

2) Although 91% of the population knew *something* about The Samaritans, many people had various misconceptions about its service: for example, 50% of people thought The Samaritans took soup and bread to down-and-outs (or did not know), and 76% of people thought The Samaritans was only a telephone service (or did not know).

Research had demonstrated a real need for clarification at a central level of The Samaritans' mission so that future communication could be more focussed.

3) The elderly, the young, the downmarket and the unemployed were significantly less aware of The Samaritans than others in the sample.

Research had highlighted an opportunity for far more effective allocation of resources and targeting of activities.

Actions Taken as a Result of the Research Findings

The actions taken by The Samaritans as a result were far-reaching. In summary, this knowledge led to:

- Re-organisation of The Samaritans' management structure.
- Formal definition of The Samaritans' positioning.
- Greater integration of the fundraising function and development of a *joint* fundraising and publicity programme to give The Samaritans a much higher profile as a charity in need of donations.
- Establishment of links with other organisations to best target specific groups in need (such as Age Concern, the NSPCC and trade unions).
- Definition and establishment of the 'Outreach' programme – the setting-up of focussed and specialised teams to reach the less aware/needy groups identified.
- Production of targeted literature, advertising and promotions.

Resultant Business Success and Conclusions

The Samaritans' reviewed activities have undoubtedly been a huge success – net funding has increased by 73% over the last year, callers from targeted groups are increasing, and there are now 8 Outreach teams with 40 members. The Samaritans has planned a further wave of research to examine changes in public attitudes for a complete picture of its success.

This paper sets out to demonstrate that by using entirely standard (and therefore cost-effective) research techniques, an organisation can identify and effectively implement radical changes to achieve outstanding results. Without the research, The Samaritans would have taken entirely different decisions; instead, it is financially in a far stronger position and its activities are far more effective.

* * * * *

WHO ARE THE SAMARITANS?

> "The primary aim of The Samaritans is to be available at any hour of the day or night to befriend those passing through personal crises and in imminent danger of taking their own lives"
>
> (First Principle)

The Samaritans is a charity founded in 1953 to offer sympathetic, caring and confidential support at any time to anyone feeling suicidal or despairing, and for whom life may be getting too much to bear. It also seeks to alleviate human misery, loneliness, despair and depression by listening to and befriending those who feel that they have no-one else to turn to who would understand and accept them. Since its inception, The Samaritans has grown as the demand for the kind of help it offers has grown; suicide rates remain high, and among certain groups are increasing, and growth in the number of new callers far outstrips growth in volunteers. Today there are 186 branches nationwide staffed by over 22,000 volunteers, receiving over two and a half million calls for help every year.

BUSINESS BACKGROUND : THE SITUATION IN 1989

In 1989 the financial position of The Samaritans was relatively poor; as a charity, it relied for its service on voluntary funds from the public, but in terms of donations received it was relatively insignificant, failing even to reach the list of the 200 largest charities (in terms of income) published annually by the Charities Aid Foundation.

At the time there was little central co-ordination or management of branch fundraising; The Samaritans had only 3 central fundraising staff, and the majority of fundraising occurred at branch level, in no structured way. The Samaritans recognised its need for more funds, and hence improved fundraising, but was concerned to find out *why* fundraising was difficult and how most effectively to increase funding; did, for example, the public think it was not in need of funds, or was less deserving than other charities? Armed with this knowledge, it could address the source of the problem, and act to change the public's perceptions first, rather than organising a less effective general programme of fundraising. The Samaritans suspected that people might not think of it as a *charity*, and hence might not realise that it was dependent on voluntary donations. Such a misconception would explain its disappointing ability to raise funds, and its relatively weak financial performance.

The positioning of The Samaritans was also in need of clarification; was it there for the suicidal, the pre-suicidal, or more widely, just as 'someone to talk to'? Historic communication on this point had varied, and there seemed to be some confusion among its own branches, let alone among the general public and the people they were trying to help. As a preface to any definition or clarification of The Samaritan's role, it was obviously essential to establish where the public's perceptions lay, to understand where and how changes were needed.

Although The Samaritans offered its help to everyone in need, irrespective of social status, age or sex, it was aware that suicide rates were higher among certain sectors of the population, such as young people and the elderly, and hence that certain groups might need its service more than others. At the time, however, there was little specific targeting of groups, central co-ordination or planning of activities directed at these groups, nor did The Samaritans have any up-to-date understanding of these groups' awareness of it. There was a growing recognition within the charity that its resources might not be targeted most effectively, to address those people who knew least about it or who needed its service most. Before making any decisions, The Samaritans needed to know how far people were aware of it and to what extent different sectors of the population understood what it could offer, as the consequences, in terms of re-direction of funds, management structure and promotional activities could be far-reaching for the organisation.

Changes to any of these three areas would potentially have a significant effect on The Samaritans and its planned strategy for the movement. Not only would any decision affect the management structure, activities and communication, but any changes would fundamentally impact on the financial position of the charity and its basic tenets. Obviously in this context, a fair and accurate understanding of the issues involved and the beliefs and attitudes of the public was essential to test hypotheses and to provide a sound base for such decisions. The Samaritans believed that such understanding could only come from carefully conducted research. As part of a programme of research, the management decided to commission research to address the following questions:

- Are people aware of The Samaritans *as a charity* and thus of its need for funds?

- Are people aware of who The Samaritans are and what they do? Are some groups less aware than others?

Research was therefore conducted in November 1989 by Audience Selection, to test the hypothesis about the public's perceptions of The Samaritans as a charity, and the more strategic study was conducted by NOP Market Research Ltd.

THE RESEARCH

The research was designed to best answer the following questions:

Audience Selection

1. How far do people recognise The Samaritans as a charity?

2. Is The Samaritans thought to be more or less desperate for money than other named charities?

3. Is The Samaritans thought to be more or less deserving than other charities?

4. Did receipt of a mailing from The Samaritans affect the replies?

NOP

1. Overall, to what extent are people aware of what The Samaritans does?

2. Is The Samaritans seen more as a 'rescuing' organisation than a 'preventing' one?

3. Do people believe that national or local government departments fund The Samaritans?

A telephone omnibus survey was felt to be the most appropriate and efficient method of research for testing the first set of hypotheses. The second set of questions seemed to be more complex, require greater probing on the part of the interviewer and provide a greater volume of information, so face-to-face interviewing in-home was seen to be the most effective method of data collection, maximising the quality of the answers.

Quantitative rather than qualitative research was commissioned to establish the prevalence of attitudes amongst the population with statistical validity. It was important to cover as wide a sample as possible, therefore both studies consisted of large samples systematically selected to be representative of the population.

METHODOLOGY

This paper sets out to demonstrate that entirely standard (and therefore cost-effective) research techniques can be used effectively to influence and change decisions. The methodology described is similar to the majority of the research conducted in the UK, but as we will see, had an enormous impact on the charity.

Audience Selection

1,023 adults aged 15+ were interviewed as part of Audience Selection's 'phonebus'(telephone omnibus) survey between 10-12 November 1989. The survey was based on a representative sample of adults; telephone households were selected at random from telephone directories covering the whole of Great Britain, and set quota controls were imposed within region, by age within sex and social class within sex. Supervision of the interviews was carried out throughout the fieldwork period.

NOP Market Research Ltd

1,966 adults aged 15+ were interviewed in their homes between 15-20 November 1989. Respondents were selected from the electoral register according to a systematic probability sample designed to be representative of all adults in Great Britain, as it was essential to minimise the possibility of sampling errors for such a major strategic study.

A technical appendix contains sampling details.

KEY RESEARCH FINDINGS

With the help of the questionnaires a large amount of information was sought and collected, and only the key findings are presented here.

1) Awareness of The Samaritans as a charity, needing public financial support, was very low:

- Only 1.4% of respondents mentioned The Samaritans as a charity they could think of.

Figure 1 Awareness of Charities
"Which charities can you think of?" (spontaneous)

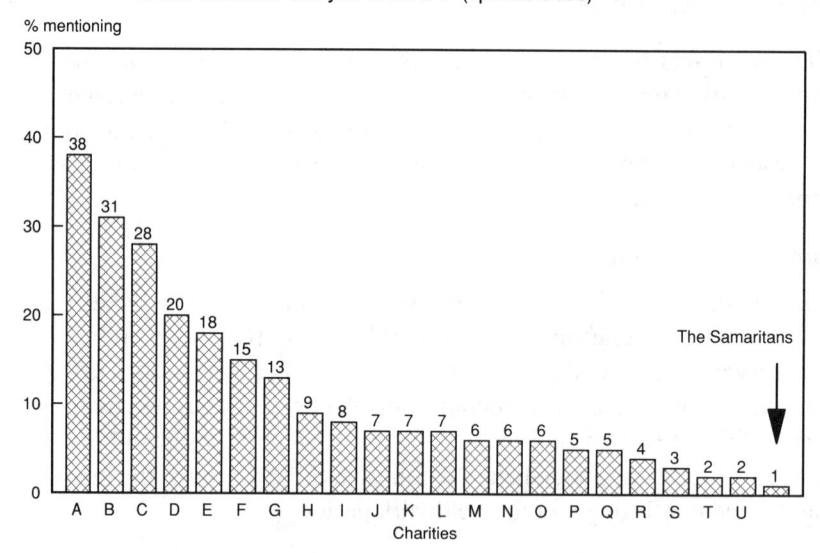

Charity	% mentioning
A	38
B	31
C	28
D	20
E	18
F	15
G	13
H	9
I	8
J	7
K	7
L	7
M	6
N	6
O	6
P	5
Q	5
R	4
S	3
T	2
U (The Samaritans)	2
	1

Base: 1,023 adults
Source: Audience Selection

The Samaritans

- 16% of people believed that "The Samaritans gets most of its money from the Government/Social Services/Local Councils" and 38% did not know; less than half the population (46%) realised The Samaritans relies mainly on funding by the public.

- The Samaritans was seen to be somewhat less desperate for money from the general public than other charities, although not less deserving. However, the level of 'don't knows' was higher than that for any other charity mentioned – a surprisingly large number of people just did not know how much The Samaritans was in need of money.

- However, those people who claimed to have received a fundraising mailing from The Samaritans appeared to be significantly more aware of what The Samaritans is and does. For example, 76% disagreed with "The Samaritans gets most of its money from the Government/Social Services/Local Councils", compared to 46% overall.

2) Positioning:

Although 91% of the population knew *something* about The Samaritans, many people had various misconceptions about its service. For example, 50% of people thought The Samaritans took soup and bread to down-and-outs (or did not know), and 76% of people thought The Samaritans was only a telephone service (or did not know). There were also differences of degree – from advising to listening to people's problems, to helping the suicidal – all of which were a concern for The Samaritans.

3) Targeting:

- The elderly, the young, the downmarket and the unemployed were significantly less aware of The Samaritans than others in the sample.

- Not only did up to 20% of these groups not know at all what The Samaritans did, but many more also thought that The Samaritans performed quite different services. To take one example; among those aged 71+, 25% said The Samaritans take soup and bread to down-and-outs, and 40% did not know (24% and 26% overall). 10% said The Samaritans decorate old people's houses for them. 47% did not know (9% and 31% overall).

10   Research Works

Figure 2   Those who do not know what The Samaritans do

"I'd like you to think about an organisation called The Samaritans. In your own words, what do you imagine they actually do?"

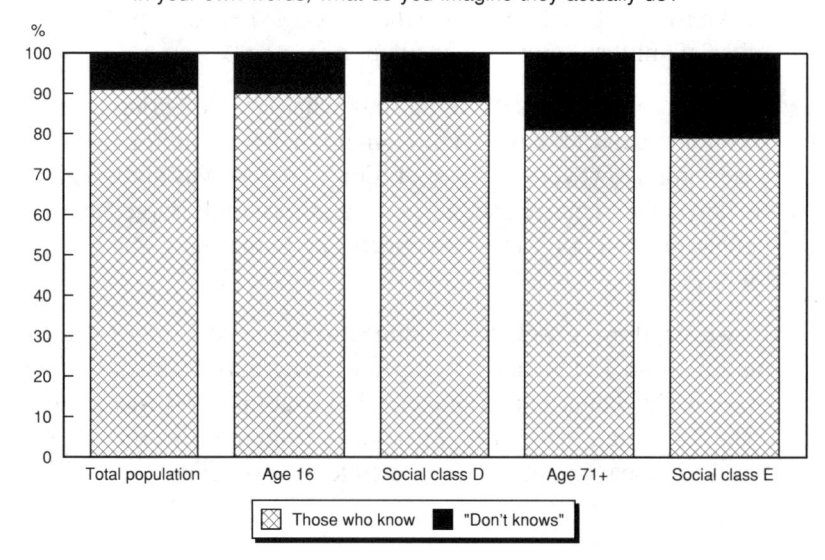

[Bar chart showing percentages of "Those who know" vs "Don't knows":
- Total population: ~90% know, ~10% don't know
- Age 16: ~90% know, ~10% don't know
- Social class D: ~87% know, ~13% don't know
- Age 71+: ~81% know, ~19% don't know
- Social class E: ~79% know, ~21% don't know]

Legend: ☒ Those who know   ■ "Don't knows"

Base: 1,966 adults
Source: NOP Market Research

IMPLICATIONS OF RESEARCH FINDINGS

1) As The Samaritans had begun to suspect, a large number of the population, although they might be aware of The Samaritans and its service, were not aware of it *as a charity*. A large sector of the public therefore apparently did not realise that it relied on donations from the public for the funding of its service. For The Samaritans this was a startling finding, putting into perspective its difficulty in raising funds from the general public; as the Director of Fundraising put it:

> "We knew we were not front of mind as a charity
> – we don't pay our volunteers, we don't charge our
> callers. But we had no idea how *few* people saw us
> as a charity".

It seemed that the public would need to be re-educated and that the fundraising structure and activities would have to be reassessed, and the emphasis shifted. Research had isolated the specific problem; the need was not purely for increased fundraising activities (similar to banging their heads against a brick wall!), but for a programme of awareness of The Samaritans and its need for money in conjunction with concentrated targeting of fundraising activities.

2) In terms of positioning, although the research showed that people's impressions and beliefs about The Samaritans' service had moved in a positive direction compared with 5 years previously, it was apparent that there was still a real need for clarification at a central level of The Samaritans' mission so that future communication could be more focussed.

3) The lack of awareness of The Samaritans and understanding of its service was also a concern. Although, encouragingly, 91% of the population as a whole did know something about The Samaritans, there were significant misconceptions about what it did, as we have seen, which for such a vital service was worrying. More worrying still, of course, was the finding of relative ignorance of The Samaritans amongst the elderly, the young, the downmarket and the unemployed. As these were the people most at risk from the problems The Samaritans was most qualified to help, these gaps were obviously going to require urgent attention, in terms of money, time and resources.

ACTIONS TAKEN AS A DIRECT RESULT OF THE FINDINGS OF THE RESEARCH

The actions taken by The Samaritans on the basis of the understanding gained from the research were extensive. To summarise briefly, this knowledge resulted in:

- Reorganisation of The Samaritans' management structure.

- Definition of The Samaritans' positioning.

- Greater integration of the fundraising function and development of a fundraising/education programme to give The Samaritans a much higher profile as a charity in need of donations.

- Establishment of links with other organisations to best target specific groups in need.

- Establishment of sponsored 'Outreach' positions and focussed teams to reach these less aware/needy groups.

The research findings were key in effecting these changes to The Samaritans' organisation and activities. In recognition of the value of such research in clarifying its objectives, confirming courses of action and identifying new needs and opportunities, The Samaritans has planned a further wave of research to examine changes in public attitudes and hence the success of its actions.

SPECIFIC INITIATIVES

Fundraising

Having identified such a low awareness of its fundraising needs, The Samaritans took immediate action, instigating a programme of regular fundraising press releases to start to raise awareness of the need for funds, and a National Fundraising Day at branch level. The fundraising day aimed to stimulate and encourage local branches to organise informative fundraising events in their local communities, and was so successful that it is now planned as an annual event, linked to the press releases, as a focus for local fundraising activities.

The Samaritans also began to include as a matter of policy a paragraph on fundraising in all its press releases, and to use the word 'charity' explicitly as often as possible in all its communication, its literature, posters and advertising. The success of this change in raising general awareness of its dependence on voluntary donations will be determined by the next wave of research.

As for organisation, the research findings focussed the minds of the voluntary governing body, who agreed to devote more resources to fundraising. Thus in 1988, there were three central fundraising staff; by 1990 this had doubled, and The Samaritans intends to add four more by the end of the year. It is also planning to integrate fundraising with its central office – currently the two functions are located in separate offices.

The research findings also demonstrated the complete interdependence of fundraising with publicity and PR. With this in mind, a joint Fundraising and Publicity Conference for representatives from the branches was also organised, and again is planned to be an annual event, to increase fundraising expertise at branch level. A fundraising manual has also been produced for the branches containing facts and ideas about fundraising, and providing well-defined guidance for managing fundraising, demonstrating the new approach to the branches.

The programme of fundraising mailings had originally been planned to last for three years, but their success having been demonstrated by research (76% of people who had received a mailing disagreed that The Samaritans gets most of its money from the Government, compared with 46% overall), The Samaritans has continued to invest in these mailings, and has increased the variety of information it provides. Leaflets explaining about The Samaritans and its need for funds have also been providing details of procedures for legacies, and issued to solicitors and accountants.

Positioning

The research highlighted the need for clarification of The Samaritans' positioning, and a concise definition of the people it felt it was best able to help. The Samaritans knew it wanted to be there for those who were desperate or in distress, at the end of their tether, before it was too late – i.e. the pre-suicidal, rather than only those who had already physically done something to themselves. It wanted to be seen as a preventing rather than just a 'rescuing' organisation, but equally, it wanted to make sure it was not seen as being there for anyone who just wanted to talk about their problems. Its resources were not large enough for it to be able to promote itself on as wide a positioning as 'someone to talk to'.

Towards this end, The Samaritans has developed a word list of recommended and non-preferred words to be used in all communications, to emphasise the most relevant terms and prevent confusion. It has also briefed their advertising and PR agencies to develop this positioning, and recent communication reflects this.

Similarly, The Samaritans has developed policy guidelines about callers it is less able to help and who prevent resources being available for those in serious and immediate distress.

Samaritan Week (a national biannual week of activities) in 1990 included a report on The Samaritans' positioning, and the most recent annual report also reflects the current focussing on life affirmation rather than suicide. In future, The Samaritans believes that its overall positioning will be clearer, and the way it is seen by the public more focussed (as future research will hopefully show).

Targeting

With the confirmation provided by the research that certain sectors of the population, those who were known to be more at risk, were less aware of The Samaritans and its work, The Samaritans began to develop two major initiatives to reach them.

The first involved establishing links with other organisations in close contact with and with experience of these groups of people, in order to reach them quickly. Developing these links and providing information to these organisations is now a major programme for The Samaritans.

The second involved the development of what the movement calls the 'Outreach' programme, the setting up of focussed and specialised teams to target The Samaritans' service in the community to those who need it most. This had existed in embryonic form, but the assurance provided by the research enabled The Samaritans to invest with confidence far more heavily in this area. The principle behind the Outreach service is that of:

> "making our service truly available, accessible and acceptable to distressed, especially suicidally distressed, people in groups which evidence suggests are particularly vulnerable, but nevertheless are under-represented among our callers".

In July 1990, The Samaritans appointed a central co-ordinator (a post sponsored by BP – another example of the success of The Samaritans' fundraising programme), and there are now 8 Outreach teams with 40 members, in addition to regional co-ordinators. It is also hoped that all branches will eventually have an Outreach officer.

SPECIFIC NEW ACTIVITIES TARGETED AT THESE GROUPS

The Elderly

In addition to the work of the Elderly Outreach team, a major programme of communication has been instigated to target those above retirement age as both callers and volunteers. Leaflets specifically for the elderly have been printed, illustrating The Samaritans' understanding of their particular problems.

The Samaritans has also started advertising in magazines targeting the elderly, such as the Saga magazine *Choice*, BUPA's *Upbeat*, and the *Management Retirement Guide*. Large print bookmarks have also been printed, and The Samaritans has initiated an organised programme of promotional activity, contributing to retirement conferences and providing literature to mobile libraries, for example.

Finally, The Samaritans has made contact with other organisations in close contact with the elderly, such as Age Concern, WRVS, the WI, the Red Cross, and health visitors, helping with training, providing speakers, literature and support.

In addition, other Outreach teams are aware of the needs and special problems of the elderly, and to some extent overlap – such as the Hospital Outreach, Rural Outreach and Events Outreach.

Young People

A wide variety of activities has been organised to raise awareness of The Samaritans among young people. The Samaritans has always been concerned about the needs and problems of young people, but since 1989, a co-ordinated programme has been far more fully developed, and investment of resources in this area significantly increased.

A programme for schools has been developed together with a Resource Pack for teachers – a new departure for The Samaritans, who had never specifically contacted people below fifth-form level and 1,300 resource packs have been sent out in the first two months. A pilot project involving centrally funded youth workers (the funding obtained from Telethon) working in schools has also been set up in Central London, with the intention of expanding the programme to other inner city areas. As a consequence of its recent work and involvement in this area, The Samaritans is now included in the national curriculum, on the Social and Moral Education curriculum, with the aim of raising awareness and understanding of life issues with young people.

The Samaritans has increased its advertising in youth magazines, including student magazines, *19*, *Just 17* and *Guiding* magazine, encouraging both young callers and attracting volunteers. Recent awareness about youth suicide in the media has also been aided by The Samaritans, together with articles about the movement.

A new cinema commercial has been developed depicting a young girl, *Saira*. The Samaritans had used the cinema as a medium before – separate research had shown it to be effective – but never specifically showing a young person. The research alerted The Samaritans to the need for effectively reaching a young audience so that it re-examined both its use of media and the content of its advertising.

The Samaritans has also forged formal and informal links with the NSPCC, National Children's Home, Childline, the Youth Club Federation and the YMCA, to encourage referrals. It has also developed its links with Nightline, the on-campus students' helpline, training Nightline volunteers.

And again, the young are now covered by other specific Outreach teams, particularly Events' Outreach. There is also a Mobile Befriending Centre and a new Promotion Unit (a specially designed vehicle funded by British Telecom) for use at major events attended by young people. These vehicles attend events which may attract distressed or lonely people, such as pop concerts, festivals or Trafalgar Square on New Year's Eve, where emotional support can be offered.

The 'Downmarket'/Unemployed

As this is obviously a diverse group, a number of teams have been developed for these and other specific groups in need – obviously the programmes for the elderly and youth will reach some of these people, but also such teams as Prison Outreach and Rural Outreach.

Links have also been formed with individual trade unions and the TUC, and with 'agony aunts' from mass media newspapers and magazines, who have been provided with specially produced leaflets to send out to people who might need to contact The Samaritans. Literature has also been produced for the use of professionals coming into contact with these groups, who could tell people about, or refer people to, The Samaritans – such as social workers, health visitors, probation officers and doctors.

Finally, advertising for and articles about The Samaritans appear more and more frequently in widely-read media (*The Sun*, *Living*, *Me*, *Best*, *Bella*, and *Chat*, for example), and on buses and tubes.

In summary, The Samaritans has thought carefully about the findings that certain groups in society are less aware of it and its work, and has set up and developed a carefully-targeted and integrated programme to address the gaps, encompassing focussed teams of visiting Outreach officers, targeted programmes of publicity and the establishment and development of close links with other organisations with experience in these areas. All branches are also now involved with Outreach.

RESULTANT BUSINESS SUCCESS

Fundraising

The Samaritans' reviewed fundraising activities have been a striking success – net fundraising has increased by 73% over the last year, and The Samaritans is now 168th on the Charities Aid Foundation list of charities in order of voluntary income.

Figure 3   Fundraising Income
An increase of 73%

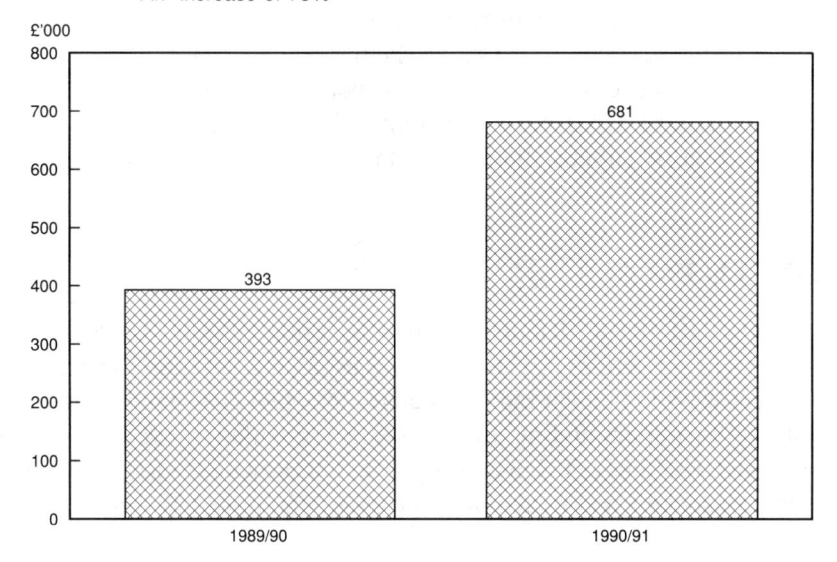

£'000
- 1989/90: 393
- 1990/91: 681

Source: The Samaritans

An additional measure of success to be established by the next wave of research will be the extent to which people's perceptions of The Samaritans as a charity in need of funds have increased.

Positioning

The Samaritans has also formally defined and clarified its positioning centrally, carefully thinking through and developing a word list of recommended terms to eliminate misunderstanding or inconsistency in communication. How far this has been successful will again be determined by the research examining the public's and, specifically, callers' perceptions. The Samaritans hopes that the public's beliefs about it and its services will be clearer and more accurate.

Fundamentally, however, research prompted The Samaritans to act in this difficult and sensitive area, and alerted it to the need for long-term planning and management of its role.

Targeting

There are now 8 Outreach teams with 40 members working in the community to promote awareness of The Samaritans and help the targeted groups identified. The Samaritans will be able to monitor the numbers of new callers from these groups to evaluate how successful the programme has been, and research will also show whether awareness and understanding of The Samaritans for these sectors of the population have increased.

The Samaritans' success in establishing links with other organisations and its production of targeted literature and advertising is also a great step forward.

CONCLUSION

This paper sets out to demonstrate that by using entirely standard (and therefore cost-effective) research techniques, an organisation can identify and effectively implement radical changes to achieve outstanding results. Without the understanding of the issues provided by research The Samaritans would have taken entirely different decisions; instead, it is far stronger financially and its activities are clearly far more effective.

APPENDICES

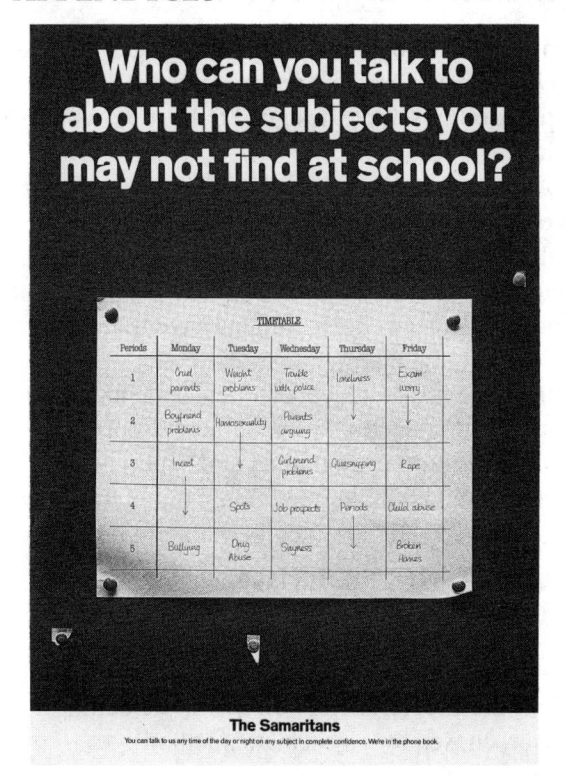

Advertising targeted towards the youth

A still from *Saira*

NOP MARKET RESEARCH TECHNICAL NOTE

NOP Market Research Limited carried out a survey of adults aged 15 years and over, between 15-20 November 1989. The respondents were selected according to a systematic probability sample designed to be representative of all adults in Great Britain.

An overall success rate of 50% was achieved (excluding electors who had died or moved away at the time of the survey) and, in total, 1,966 interviews took place with adults aged 15+.

The sample of non-electors has been weighted to bring it into line with the sample of electors. In addition inter-cellular weights have been applied and weighted.

As many as four recalls were made to contact respondents and no substitutes were taken. Completed interviews were subject to a 10% field check. Interviewing was carried out by fully trained and supervised NOP Market Research interviewers.

TECHNICAL NOTE ON SAMPLE DESIGN AND WEIGHTING METHODS

The sample used was a two-stage, stratified random sample, electors' names being drawn at random from the Electoral Register (with the addition of non-electors aged 15 and over, chosen by a systematic method).

The Sample Design

Constituencies

631 parliamentary constituencies in Great Britain were classified into the Registrar General's ten Standard Regions. Within each standard Region constituencies were classified into four types:

i) Metropolitan County*

ii) Other 100% urban

iii) Mixed urban/Rural

iv) Rural

Within the resultant cells, constituencies were listed according to the percentage of people resident in households whose head is in socio-economic groups 1, 2, 3, 4 or 13. A systematic sample of 180 constituencies was taken with the probability of selection proportional to the size of the electorate in each constituency.

Electors

Within each constituency a random elector was selected, who became the first elector of a cluster. To form a cluster every fifteenth elector was selected following the first randomly selected elector until the required number of electors had been reached.

The standard national cluster size was set at eighteen. Constituencies presenting special peculiarities (those within the old GLC area and a small number of others within the London ITV Area) were allocated an average augmented cluster of thirty, increased to fifty in exceptional circumstances.

The sample comprised 3,560 named electors drawn from the Electoral Register of the selected constituencies. Interviewers were instructed to call and recall on these named electors, in order to obtain interviews with as high a proportion as possible. No substitutes were taken.

Non-Electors

A sample of non-electors aged 15 and over was also interviewed. At the household of each selected elector, each interviewer inquired whether there were any non-electors aged 15 and over in the household. If there was one, he or she was interviewed (in addition to the elector). If there was more than one such non-elector, the interviewer listed their names alphabetically by surname and then by first name and selected one at random using a Kish selection grid. Thus one interview with a non-elector aged 15 and over was attempted at each household where they occurred. No substitutes were taken.

Recalls were made to secure interviews with the selected non-electors.

Weighting Methods

Non-electors – The sample of non-electors was given the following weight:

$$\frac{\text{No. of Non-Electors in Household}}{\text{No. of names on Register leading to the Household}}$$

In addition, weights were applied derived from the following demographic characteristics:

- Male/Female.
- 15-24/25-34/35-44/45-54/55-90/60-64/65-70/71+.

- A/B/C1/C2/D/E.
- North Yorkshire and Humberside/East Midlands/East Anglia/GLC/South East excluding GLC*/South West/Wales/Scotland.
- Twelve ITV Areas, according to November 1986 ITCA definitions.

* Definition prior to abolition on 1st April 1986.

2

ROYAL MAIL

FROM PILLAR-BOX TO DOOR-MAT

SUMMARY

Long before John Major and his advisors ever coined the term *Citizens' Charter*, several public service businesses, including Royal Mail, had already made significant progress in improving service quality. Although they lacked overt competition, they realised that complacency would sound the death-knell for their businesses. In the case of Royal Mail, telephone, fax and couriers were becoming more of a threat in a marketplace where the reliable and predictable transmission of communications was not a request but an expectation.

Until three years ago, Royal Mail's Quality of Service monitor was based on an internal measure which timed the transit of letters from arrival in the sorting office to the time they were ready to be delivered. Because of its two obvious drawbacks – ignoring collection or delivery failures, and perceived lack of independence – it came under attack by both competitors and critics. The bad press that ensued did nothing to enhance Royal Mail's credibility with its customers.

In 1988, Royal Mail decided that a new survey was required to measure reality as it is experienced by its customers – in other words, the time taken from the posting of a letter in the pillar-box to its arrival on the door-mat.

Accordingly, a large scale, continuous research monitor was developed by Royal Mail in conjunction with Research International. It is known as the 'End-to-End' survey. Although complex in design and execution, the principles that under-pin it are simple: panels of customers post test letters to each other, the agency measures transit times, then calculates the percentage of letters meeting the target delivery day. This percentage is what is generally referred to as the 'Quality of Service'.

The End-to-End survey is now viewed widely as the single most important tool for measuring Royal Mail's success in meeting customer needs. Additionally, it is instrumental in determining key staff bonuses and also forms part of the 'Public Record'.

Given the uses to which the survey is put, it is not surprising that it is subject to exceedingly high standards for sampling, fieldwork, analysis and reporting. The agency and Royal Mail work closely together to set and re-set improvement targets for the quality of the data.

The End-to-End survey has had a profound impact on Royal Mail's business.

Over the past three years, overall Quality of Service has improved by eleven percentage points.

Royal Mail is now able to boast that it offers the best and most reliable postal service in Europe. Not only are comparative Quality of Service figures very favourable, but other postal administrations are also in discussion with Royal Mail to copy the End-to-End methodology.

The improvements in the End-to-End performance have undoubtedly eased the passage of tariff increases, enabling Royal Mail to invest in improving quality still further.

Apart from providing overall measures of performance, the survey is used diagnostically to highlight particular problem areas within each of Royal Mail's sixty-three Districts. A whole raft of local initiatives has been prompted by reference to the End-to-End findings.

The End-to-End survey has facilitated the introduction of a Total Quality Management programme throughout Royal Mail. Staff have metamorphosed: the old production-led philosophy has been replaced by an external-facing performance orientation.

In short, this is a story of a considerable research investment by a public sector organisation which, by taking the findings to heart and acting on them, is allowing the customer to reap substantial benefits.

*   *   *   *   *

INTRODUCTION: IMPETUS FOR CHANGE

Both Conservative and Labour parties have recently put forward preliminary ideas for a *Citizens' Charter*, the purpose of which would be to improve the lot of the consumers of public services. Extensive media coverage has fuelled the debate with advocates from the right and left attempting to make their voices heard above the hype of those who, for whatever reason, have now jumped on the band-wagon.

The debate hinges on the fear that lack of competition in the public sector may lead to complacency in dealings with the man in the street (the 'customer'). Those on the right of the political spectrum complain that, unlike service industries operating in the free market, public services do not need to make the same efforts in order to win or retain customers. Those on the left tend to concern themselves more with the rights of the paying public to enjoy consistently high levels of service in their dealings with the state, or with state corporations.

Whatever one's political hue, there seems to be a ground-swell of opinion to place public services under increasing scrutiny, not only in terms of the cost of service provision, but also in terms of what services should be provided and how. Everyone is wanting the same attention to quality from public service providers that they now expect from the private sector.

What the media hype tends to overlook is the fact that several public service businesses, including Royal Mail, had already made significant inroads in the area of quality before John Major and his advisors ever coined the term *Citizens' Charter*.

THE CHANGING COMMUNICATIONS MARKET

Whilst Royal Mail enjoys the privilege of a monopoly on the collection and delivery of letters and small packets below the price of £1, there is no monopoly on the transmission of messages. Telephone, fax, couriers and hand delivery are all competitors in the wider marketplace. Customers expect reliable and predictable quality of service for their communications, even if speed as such is not of the essence.

Until three years ago, Royal Mail's Quality of Service monitor was based on an internal measure, which timed the transit of letters from their first arrival in the sorting office to the time that they were ready for delivery.

There were two major drawbacks to this monitor. First, it ignored any collection or delivery failures; second, since it was operated internally, it was not seen as being independent – could the data be trusted?

Taking each of these drawbacks in turn, it will be shown how the current measure evolved.

Royal Mail's ultimate 'shareholder' is the Government, through the Department of Trade and Industry (DTI). The DTI funds the Post Office Users' National Council (POUNC), which represents the interests of all Post Office customers, including those of Royal Mail. POUNC, and other consumer bodies, such as the Consumers' Association, conducted their own surveys, sometimes based on very small samples, which measured the time it took from a letter being posted, to the time it was delivered to the recipient. Since these surveys were not measuring the same thing as Royal Mail's monitor, the results were, obviously, different. But these discrepancies did nothing to enhance Royal Mail's credibility with its customers or to enable it to counter claims (often spurious) made by its competitors and critics.

Although the internal survey was designed, conducted, and controlled by professional statisticians, cynical outsiders could still claim that Royal Mail's measurement system was not independent and that the results could be 'fudged'.

Concurrently with these concerns, the management of Royal Mail wanted to bring in an incentive scheme in all sixty-three Districts linked to meeting Quality of Service improvement targets. They also wanted to develop procedures to test and partially audit operational factors; and, incidentally, to obtain diagnostic information: for example, was poor Quality of Service a result, in particular circumstances, of collection, transit or delivery problems.

Overall, the need for a new system of measuring Quality of Service was a culmination of a number of factors:

- The need for a new realism in Royal Mail's dealings with its customers.

- The imperative for independent measurement.

- A measure which would enable Districts to be set, and rewarded for meeting, improvement targets as part of a continuous programme of quality improvement.

- The need to show that the monopoly privilege was not being abused.

- The need to counteract spurious claims by competitors and to maintain Royal Mail's competitive advantage.

REQUIREMENTS OF THE SURVEY

The over-riding objective for any new survey was to measure reality as it is experienced by Royal Mail's customers, that is, from the time of posting ('Pillar-box') to the time of delivery ('Door-mat').

Additionally, the design of the new survey needed to:

- Be acceptable to the DTI, POUNC and other consumer bodies.
- Have credibility with Districts (since bonuses would depend on it).
- Provide usable data to Royal Mail management.
- Be conducted independently.
- Be subject to stringent quality control.

It was of utmost concern that the data not only be reliable from a research point of view, but also be viewed as credible by Royal Mail's owners, customers and critics. Indeed, the very public nature of the research could not be under-estimated; POUNC and the DTI scrutinise performance versus targets in great detail. Moreover, the data are published in the Post Office's Annual Report and Accounts, so form part of the 'Public Record'.

In short, the survey design and execution had to be perfect; even a small oversight could undermine the whole exercise.

OUTLINE OF RESEARCH DESIGN

The principles behind the End-to-End survey are very simple:

- Panels of customers using both stamps and meters are established.
- Panellists post test letters to each other.
- Data are captured by the agency.
- Transit times are measured.
- Quality of Service scores are calculated as a percentage meeting target delivery day.

The research design and execution are of course much more complex than this deceptively simple outline may suggest. A dedicated team of more than twenty full-time staff are required to run this survey, plus large numbers of part-time field interviewers, progress clerks, despatch clerks, telephone interviewers, and data entry staff.

In its first three years, the survey has covered all Royal Mail's sixty-three letter Districts, the target letters to be generated requiring matching to real traffic flows. This means that actual data on weight of traffic flows within Districts, to adjacent Districts, and further afield are used to set targets both for letters posted in each sub-District (an average of four per District) and for letters received in each. These flows have to be matched for both first and second class mail, and within each of these for four streams: business to business, business to private, private to business, and private to private.

The posting and delivery points to be used also have to be representative of known posting patterns. Addresses of private and business customers to be used on the panels have to be a very close match to 'ideal postcodes' selected at random from the Postcode Address File. These postcodes are rolled over on average twice a year to prevent any risk of identification of these points by Royal Mail personnel. In any one month about 3,200 individual delivery addresses are covered, each receiving between six and ten test letters. Thus, in the course of a year, over a quarter of a million items are despatched, analysed and reported on in this survey.

There are several other criteria governing the sampling. The operation is required to cover large and small envelopes. Days of the week, weeks of the month, and times of day of posting must also be representative of actual posting patterns for live mail. The proportion of private letters posted at Post Offices and in postboxes is carefully controlled.

A final important point on the size and scope of the survey is that we are aiming to measure letters 'correctly' posted. Royal Mail publish and advertise many guidelines on how to 'Get the Most from your Post'; for example, regarding the latest acceptance times for post to particular destinations, the use of postcodes and correct addressing, correct sorting of mail into first and second class pouches, and so on. There seems little point in systematically measuring and reporting on the poorer 'performance' which will obviously ensue from non-compliance with these guidelines. However, from time to time, experimental ad hoc surveys are undertaken to assess the effect of this.

Analysis is also complex and detailed. Although the survey is designed to be representative of traffic flows, there are minimum numbers of items assigned to many of the very small sub-samples of interest, which require statistical correction (or 'weighting') to return them to their true proportions at the analysis stage. Full analyses are produced on both weighted and unweighted data for the month, and on weighted data for three months, twelve months, and the year to date. Other special analyses are regularly required: data with and without the recently introduced Sunday Collections; with different geographical breakdowns to reflect re-organisation within Royal Mail; and re-adjustments to take account of changes in traffic flows over time.

This level of detail is required because of the close scrutiny to which the results are subjected, by people whose annual remuneration may depend on their success in having improved one or more of their fourteen Quality of Service targets.

A WORD ON QUALITY CONTROL

Most sample surveys are carried out with an assumption, explicit or implicit, about acceptable levels of non-sampling error. Most clients probably trust that these will be small, but accept that there will be a number of minor keying errors, routing mistakes by interviewers, etc. and that these are (generally) 'swings-and-roundabouts' in terms of the accuracy of the final results.

The End-to-End survey is not like that! There are several features which result in much higher standards of accuracy and quality requirements than for 'normal' survey research.

One example of the unusually high standards demanded of the survey is that the system allows for individual letter by letter scrutiny by the end-user. Districts have complete listings of all letters analysed with full details except exactly who the poster and receiver of each letter are. When bonuses could be affected (even jobs?) District Head Postmasters ask questions like "Are the agency sure this letter posted on Saturday in Cardiff at 10:30 a.m. would have made the latest collection time, since 9:45 is the latest collection time for much of the rural area?" A whole department and computer system are devoted to the resolution of the numerous queries like this from Districts.

The agency and Royal Mail work together to set and re-set improvement targets for the quality of the data with regard to the response rate (not all letters put in the system are returned/can be used for analysis), the accuracy with which panellists follow our instructions, and a dozen or so other criteria. These are reported on monthly, and again a whole team and computer system are devoted to the measurement and control of panellist performance, checking the output of the computer sampling program, evaluating the speed of query resolution, and other items to be measured against improvement targets.

There is a 100% manual edit of letter forms in order to validate the information by comparison with the envelope (e.g. is the postage at the correct rate?).

Panellists are monitored monthly using a purpose-built Computer Assisted Telephone Interviewing (CATI) system to facilitate panel roll-over, rapid feedback of new instructions, and queries from new panellists.

This survey is even subject to external audit by Ernst and Young – the Post Office's own auditors. This is the only example of which we are aware (though our readers may know otherwise) of a sample survey being subjected to a full and very detailed audit. The auditors examine the whole of our system in great depth, have gone back to our raw data, and tried (successfully!) to reproduce our findings.

As a result, there is not in this survey any space for even minimal levels of coding or data entry error, for occasional lapses in editing or minor errors at the analysis stage.

IMPACT OF THE SURVEY ON ROYAL MAIL'S BUSINESS

Very significant improvements in Quality of Service have been achieved since the introduction of the End-to-End survey, as the figures below show:

Table 1   % First Class letters delivered by next working day

	1989	1990	1991
Local	86	89	93
Neighbouring	75	81	87
Long Distance	65	68	79
TOTAL	75	78	86

In a recent press release, the Post Office Chairman Sir Bryan Nicholson was able to announce that the Royal Mail provides the best and most reliable postal service in Europe:

> "The Royal Mail is the only European postal administration with a major programme in place directly targeted at improving quality of service. Over the next five years we plan a record investment programme of more than £1.6 billion... We have achieved considerable and consistent improvements in recent years and we are proud of our role of best in Europe."

Not only are comparative Quality of Service figures very favourable, but other postal administrations are also in discussion with Royal Mail to copy the End-to-End methodology.

POUNC has to agree any tariff increases proposed by Royal Mail and the Council has, in the past, linked the acceptability of tariff increases with demands for improvement in the Quality of Service. The improvements made in the End-to-End performance in recent years have undoubtedly eased the passage of the tariff increases, enabling Royal Mail to invest in improving quality still further – a virtuous circle. Over the past three years the price of a first class stamp has risen from 18p to 22p and that of a second class stamp from 13p to 17p. Without an independent, reliable measure such as End-to-End, the DTI may well have faced strong pressure from POUNC to refuse, or at least reduce or delay, tariff increases. With 1990/91 letter volumes of 6,529m and 8,478m for first and second class mail respectively, even a week's delay in agreeing to a tariff increase can cost Royal Mail millions of pounds in lost revenue!

There are numerous examples of End-to-End being used to highlight particular problem areas. In Glasgow, for example, the survey was pointing to apparent collection failures. The District team found this very hard to believe, but examined the collection practices and discovered that these fell short of the laid down procedures. When procedure and practice were brought into line, there was an immediate improvement in their Quality of Service of five percentage points.

POUNC (in its Report No. 47) stated: "The Council commends the decisions by Royal Mail both to adopt the End-to-End system of measurement and to establish targets and provide data for each postal district as an indication of its commitment to tackle the quality of service problems head on."

The establishment of the End-to-End measurement as a major input to District Head Postmasters' bonuses has had the effect of enhancing the introduction of Total Quality Management throughout Royal Mail. Districts shift to a performance orientation ('what do the customers need/want?') from a procedural or production-led philosophy.

In summary, the substantial investment in End-to-End monitoring has yielded a wide range of benefits – financial, operational and in terms of the public's image of Royal Mail. Royal Mail has pride of place amongst European postal administrations, which look with envy at its Quality of Service figures.

3

HEINZ

TOWARDS MORE EFFECTIVE PROMOTIONS

SUMMARY

This paper details some ways in which Heinz have benefited from data generated by a research programme devised initially by Taylor Nelson and optimised with them. The task was to provide an evaluative framework to assist in optimising on-pack sales promotion activity.

Heinz has long been a major and highly regarded user of sales promotions as a means of generating incremental volume and creating long- and short-term interest in major brands. It has a considerable reputation amongst both manufacturers and the trade as a creative and experienced user of such activity.

Nonetheless, about six years ago Heinz felt that the time had come for a programme of research aimed at measuring the performance of particular sales promotion activities, as a means of providing guidelines for their long term optimisation. The research tools developed to meet their needs have been running in an evolving form over the last five years.

The paper describes how:

- with a consistent approach to evaluation

- and some creativity in devising a cost effective research vehicle within a tight budgetary framework there has been a considerable application by the client of new ideas generated by research into particular proven and well-tested sales promotions. Overall, we have provided a considerable return on the original investment, generating additional volume.

Heinz have traditionally run a major corporate promotion at least once a year. This paper specifically addresses the use of research on these promotions, culminating in the record breaking, prize winning Heinz 'Driveaway' promotion in 1990.

Driveaway involved:

- over 80 million promotional cans of baked beans, spaghetti products, tomato and other ready to serve soup varieties and treacle sponge pudding.
- a total prize fund of over £750,000.
- a total of 15,800 prizes over the 100 day promotional draw period.
- national and regional press advertising inviting participation in all key publications, together with a final congratulations advertisement run in the national press to thank all who participated.
- regional press/newspapers PR stories on most of the 100 car winners.
- a programme of 20 theme related, tailor-made promotions for retail and cash and carry accounts, communicated on in-store leaflets or magazine ads.

TN's research on the 1986/7/8 Heinz 'Car a Day' prize draw promotions suggested that for 1989 there could be some advantages in 'ringing the changes' – advantages that would not have been apparent from participation levels alone.

The 1989 corporate promotion – 'Write Your Own Cheque' – focused on cash prizes and achieved a number of key objectives particularly linked to changing buying behaviour. However, for a number of reasons identified by the research, it was felt that a return to a variant of the original 'Car a Day' theme would be opportune.

The resulting 1990 'Driveaway' corporate promotion set new records for Heinz:

- over eleven million promotional labels were received, over double the previous year's cash based promotion, and the largest participation yet for that style of offer.
- the research showed that, on average, seven labels were sent per entrant, that is, 1.6 million people responded to the promotion.

Some of the data provided from the evaluative research framework, on buying behaviour changes as a consequence of the promotion, were:

- over 37% of respondents changed their buying behaviour – that is nearly 450,000 entrants (and considerably more if we include those who did not send off their entry). Over one million purchases were a consequence of brand switching.
- in excess of 300,000 purchases were new trials.
- over two million purchases were consumers making a forward purchase, creating some level of stock pressure in the pantry and shutting out competitor purchase opportunities.

The promotion provided some relief to the continued pressure on Heinz core varieties from own label, and above all demonstrated to the trade the continued benefit of providing increased display space in major retail outlets.

High profile regional PR coverage, particularly focusing on the personalised DVLA Select Registration H57 Rover Metros, provided valuable media space for Heinz. The National Exhibition Centre display for the Heinz Metro 57 throughout the Annual Classic Car Show rounded off a considerable achievement by Heinz's promotional agency, Clarke Hooper.

Evaluating promotions in this way has provided Heinz with ongoing information about promotional efficacy, as well as a solid framework for immediately progressing the 1991 corporate promotional package.

Once again, Heinz and Clarke Hooper are using the research findings to fine tune specific areas for even greater success in 1991.

* * * * *

THE BUSINESS BACKGROUND

The Client – H. J. Heinz

H. J. Heinz is one of the UK's largest food manufacturers with an annual turnover of some £500 million, the majority of lines being high penetration, frequently purchased items, virtually all with market leadership. However the business environment is fiercely competitive, with pressure from other brands and own label.

To maintain and grow Heinz's consumer franchise profitably is a complex marketing and trade operations task requiring high grade, reliable intelligence to plan and execute brand support in the most efficient way.

The Heinz Philosophy

Heinz attribute their success to consistent and carefully targeted advertising and promotions linked to top quality products.

The Market Background

Heinz face continued pressure from own label on their core varieties and need increased display space in major retail outlets. Heinz Trade Operations Division works as an interface between sales and marketing and uses a small number of promotional consultancies to devise and operate a major trade marketing programme. The budget for this has grown as a share of all marketing expenditure and trebled in the last five years.

Over the last five years, starting in its Centenary year, 1986, Heinz has promoted core varieties during the key Autumn/Winter period within a major corporate promotion activity, across several major product fields.

This approach gives the opportunity to provide the customer with a single, stronger, more powerful message than could be achieved by individual brands. Of equal importance, it provides excitement and involvement on the part of the trade in the form of promotional displays and tailor-made activity.

Defining the Objectives

Like most companies with sizeable media budgets, Heinz has put considerable effort into the development, pre-testing and subsequent monitoring of their brand advertising, a process for which there has long been general acceptance of the need for a full research programme and a planning approach.

Until the mid 1980s, promotions – and specifically consumer promotions – were not given the same attention by Heinz. However, it was then recognised that the approach taken above the line was equally valid below the line, particularly given the size of Heinz's brands.

The increasing expenditure being devoted to promotions further sharpened Heinz's awareness of the need for research to be used to help deploy promotional resources to maximum effect, as well as to play a role in the promotional planning process.

Amongst other issues, Heinz needed to establish the degree to which their promotions:

- were achieving adequate levels of awareness and interest among housewives?
- were reaching the correct target market?
- were having the desired effect on purchasing?
- attracted different consumer profiles?

The Research Approach

As part of a larger project, Taylor Nelson was commissioned by Heinz in 1985 to devise a programme of research potentially applicable to a large number of different promotions, with different redemption levels, over a fairly long time period.

It was felt that conventional research approaches (personal or telephone interviewing) would quickly exhaust a finite research budget, or be very inefficient (*conventional* postal self-completion tick box/write in answers questionnaire). The method to be devised was also constrained by the non-database handling procedures used by Heinz at that time.

Taylor Nelson was conducting experimental work, including reply paid scratch-off questionnaires, to collect simple demographic data on target audiences. The attractions of the scratch-off option were that it had the benefit of being completed quickly, without the *mañana* diversion of having to find something to write with and was thought to be consonant with promotions.

Development

A self-completion questionnaire was devised with Heinz and successfully tested on three different on-pack promotions, each with a sample size of 10,000 getting an excellent average response rate of 67%. This led to a decision to save costs by halving the sample size for future surveys.

38   Research Works

To check that the non-responding minority were not significantly different from survey responders, about 1,500 non-responders were telephone interviewed (500 per promotion). Non-responders proved to be lighter ITV viewers than responders but overall there was nothing that caused concern about responder data.

Heinz were satisfied that we had come up with a cost effective solution to their needs and that the results were likely to be typical of participants in their promotions. A more detailed outline of the research method, illustrated by Figure 1 below, is provided together with Tables 1 & 2.

Figure 1   Performance evaluation – how TN PROFILE works

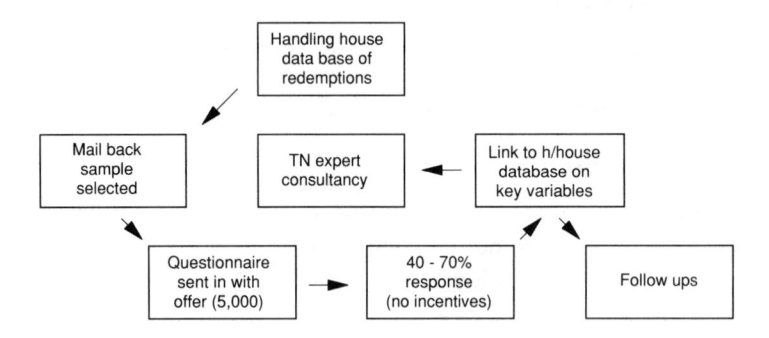

```
                    ┌─────────────────┐
                    │ Handling house  │
                    │ data base of    │
                    │ redemptions     │
                    └─────────────────┘
                           ↗     ↘
  ┌──────────┐      ┌──────────────┐      ┌──────────────┐
  │ Mail back│      │ TN expert    │ ←─── │ Link to h/house│
  │ sample   │      │ consultancy  │      │ database on  │
  │ selected │      │              │      │ key variables│
  └──────────┘      └──────────────┘      └──────────────┘
       ↘                                      ↗   ↖
  ┌──────────────┐   ┌──────────────┐   ┌──────────────┐
  │Questionnaire │   │  40 - 70%    │   │              │
  │ sent in with │ → │  response    │   │  Follow ups  │
  │ offer (5,000)│   │(no incentives)│  │              │
  └──────────────┘   └──────────────┘   └──────────────┘
```

The scene was set for an extensive and effective programme of research to cover their major types of promotion. It came at just the right time – Heinz's Centenary Year, 1986.

Evaluating the Big One

In 1986 Heinz had its Centenary Year. Clarke Hooper were briefed to produce a promotion to celebrate this event in the biggest and most profitable way – the result was 'Car a Day'.

Television advertising, then fairly unusual in support of an on-pack promotion, was used to grab attention and to stimulate interest in the then novel idea that for 100 days, it was possible to win a car a day from Heinz, plus many other prizes. In order not to be classed as a lottery, entry did not require purchase.

The TN PROFILE method was used to sample winners of secondary prizes and, as winners were drawn at random, they provided an acceptable sample of participants.

The 1986 research reassured Heinz that the participant profiles were satisfactory and the promotion was achieving acceptable levels of change in buyer behaviour. It also provided the basis for comparison with future corporate promotions.

The same evaluation method was used in 1987 and 1988, as Heinz and Clarke Hooper developed 'Car a Day'. This enabled them, through watching the outcome of our evaluations, to vary the choice of vehicle offered, the secondary prize structure and the support given to the promotion (see Table 1) against a background of *knowing* what had happened in terms of participant behaviour.

Table 1   Heinz Corporate Promotions 1986 – 1990

	1990 Driveaway	1989 WYOC	1988 Car/day	1987 Car/day	1986 Car/day
Daily Prizes	Limited Edition H57 Metro 57 road atlases 100 x £5.70 vouchers	1,310 cash prizes of £1-£1,000	Metro 10 hampers 100 x £5 vouchers 100 x £1 vouchers	Metro 500 x £1 vouchers	Mini, Metro Maestro, Montego or Rover
Other Prizes	–	3 x £10,000	–	–	3 x 13 seat minibus
Products	beans spaghetti soup sponge pudding	beans spaghetti soup sponge pudding	beans spaghetti soup	beans spaghetti soup	beans spaghetti soup sponge pudding
Promotional Support	press	limited press	press	press	TV

In each year the objective has been to get an increase in the *absolute* number of people changing their buying in favour of Heinz to take part. Therefore, the analysis takes into account both the *number* of applications and the research evidence on *how* people bought to take part. The level of non-label entries has not been such as to warrant research on them.

Entrants are Just Part of the Picture

All promotions have those who fully participate and are dealt with by the handling house. There are also those who get part way towards full participation, but for whatever reason fall by the wayside (slippage). Some become aware of the promotion message and may be influenced by it, though they do not act on it in the short term. The promotion is, after all, a brand communication.

Establishing the level of prompted awareness and response state of consumers for these corporate promotions (and other major offers) has been done by showing the relevant pack labels, among a set of labels for other offers, to housewives on our weekly random omnibus survey OMNIMAS. This has enabled Heinz to determine how promotions compare on getting awareness and how much of that awareness seems likely to convert into different response states. Is more awareness gained and more participation likely than last time?

Trends Shown by the Research

The 1987 and 1988 corporate promotions achieved identical levels of awareness and non-rejection.

However, in 1988, the evidence from the participant evaluation was that there seemed to have been a falling off in the power of the promotion to change participant buying behaviour (from 40% to 33% of participants). The answer was either to get a massive increase in the number of labels sent in, or a restoration of the power of the promotion to change behaviour. The ideal, of course, would be to get both!

How the Research Ultimately Led to a Record Breaking, Award Winning 1990 Promotion

Armed with the trends apparent from the research on 'Car a Day' 1986-88, Clarke Hooper devised a different approach for 1989 – 'Write Your Own Cheque'. Instead of offering just one major prize per day, this offered over a thousand cash prizes of up to £1,000, with a chance to win one of three £10,000 prizes over the three month period.

Evaluation of the 1989 'Write Your Own Cheque' promotion showed that it generated only two thirds of the awareness generated by previous corporate promotions, although among those aware of it, proportionately more considered that they would do something with it. This did generate a return to the greater change in buying behaviour among participants seen in the initial Heinz corporate promotions.

However, when the number of applications was taken into account (see Table 2), the outcome was less gratifying in the *absolute* number of buyers changing their buying.

Cash appeared to be less attention getting than cars but more influential on those prepared to consider it.

Table 2   Number of labels estimated to come from different buying response states among promotion participants 1986-90

millions of labels *	labels	changed buying total changed	new variety	switched brand	stocked up	bought as usual
1990 Driveaway	11.2	3.4	0.34	1.01	2.35	7.84
1989 Write Your Own Cheque	5.4	2.3	0.16	0.65	1.62	3.13
1988 Car a Day	6.4	2.1	0.13	0.51	1.60	4.28
1987 Car a Day	6.1	2.4	0.18	0.37	1.95	3.66
1986 Car a Day	5.9	2.5	0.35	0.53	1.77	3.36

Note: *some multiple answers

So the key objectives for 1990 were:

- to get a higher level of awareness
- without being seen to be a stale return to 'Car a Day'
- so that the benefits of higher awareness could be coupled with a lower level of rejection to produce more entries
- and a return to the earlier levels of the ability of the promotion to induce change in buying behaviour, generating a substantial increase in the *number* of people changing their buying behaviour when participating.

The creative solution devised by Clarke Hooper was to return to the familiar 'Car a Day' format – but to take advantage of a personalized prize car and the opportunity offered by the 'H' registration year. This meant that the promotion could offer limited special edition Rover Metro '57's, including logo branding, sun-roof and central locking, *plus*, through the DVLA 'Select Registration' number scheme, unique H57 six digit personalised registrations (e.g. H57 MJD – these were the *only* H57 registrations issued). Such unique prizes were correctly thought likely to capture valuable media interest and to create massive interest in the trade – they would also provide the key point of difference from previous Heinz 'Car a Day' promotions. Secondary prizes were 57 Heinz/AA Road Atlases and 100 £5.70 Heinz vouchers, per day. It was called 'Driveaway'.

Over 80 million promotional cans were produced and major retail outlets were supplied with headboards and shelf edgers.

National and regional press advertising invited participation in all key publications and regional newspapers carried PR stories on most of the 100 winners.

The Outcome for 'Driveaway'

- awareness of the promotion was significantly boosted (by six percentage points on 'Write Your Own Cheque'), as was interest in taking part (up over a third on 'Write Your Own Cheque'), so that 'Driveaway' achieved the desired combination of the high awareness seen on earlier 'Car a Day' promotions and the higher interest level of 'Write Your Own Cheque', leading to an expectation of high application levels.

- the number of labels sent in was *over double* the 1989 level and a new record.

- however, the proportion of applicants who changed their buying behaviour was not as high as had been hoped.

- nevertheless, because the number of applications was so enormous, the absolute estimated number of applications from those changing their buying behaviour was dramatically higher than ever before (see Table 2).

Incidentally, there was an over 80% response level for the PROFILE questionnaires.

Heinz had their most successful ever promotion for this style of offer, with over 11 million labels received. We estimate from our evaluation findings that these came from approximately 1.6 million people, 27% of whom changed their buying behaviour in Heinz's favour to take part – that's nearly 450,000 consumers.

This promotion won an Award of Excellence (Best Usage Programme) for Clarke Hooper at the 1991 Council of Sales Promotion Agencies international awards ceremony – the only British winner. It was the winner of the 1990 Promotional Techniques Award from the Institute of Sales Promotions.

The Future

Heinz work to an 18 month promotional planning cycle and the main promotional vehicle – the pack labels – requires artwork 9-20 weeks before sell-in across as many as 80 different sizes and varieties. Critical decisions on this year's major corporate promotion were being taken within a few weeks of the research debrief on last year's version.

Research innovations included in 1990 will be repeated, including questions on which of the Heinz Corporate promotions applicants have entered and how many times they have entered the current promotion. Consideration may be given to data capture of the labels sent in by respondents, to provide additional depth to the analysis.

Meanwhile, we continue adding to Heinz's knowledge of how their other promotions perform, with new issues being covered and new insights gained by comparison with the considerable amount of analysis already done.

APPENDICES

An Outline of the Research Method

The research procedure is illustrated in Figure 1. 5,000 reply paid questionnaires are usually provided to the handling house. Content is tailored to the specific needs of the promotion, but core questions are retained for comparability.

The questionnaire is sealable when folded, for security. Responses are printed on scratch-off foil to reveal the same answers when the appropriate answer boxes are 'scratched off'.

High production standards are used, as would be expected of our client, and the questionnaire is endorsed by their logo. An integral explanation section, as from the client, removes the need for a separate letter.

We jointly agree on when the questionnaires are to be sent out in a sample of the mailback packs (e.g. with the product purchase vouchers) to promotion applicants by the handling house.

Typically, the questionnaires are sent out to the 'next 5,000 applicants' at about the peak flow of applications, as regularly monitored by the handling house. The sampling is effectively random as the applications are processed unsorted.

In some cases, where applications are data captured, arrangements can be made to enter the serial number of the questionnaire sent to each applicant. This is so that the handling house data for that applicant (e.g. make up of proofs of purchase, source of entry coupon etc.) can be included in the analysis and to provide a link to names and addresses. Where additional applicant data are included, we always ask that Data Protection Act requirements are met by the handling house.

When the applicant receives their mailback pack, he or she is probably at their most willing to complete the enclosed PROFILE questionnaire (the gratification effect is recognised but is less relevant when *comparing* the results of such studies). Everything is made simple for the recipient – no pen is needed, no stamp has to be found, and we do not find it necessary to offer an incentive. Recipients quickly complete and return their questionnaires to TN (not the handling house).

Data entry is followed by analysis and presentation of the findings, comparison being made where possible with:

- past promotions evaluated for the client.

- brand profile data to compare and contrast with promotion participant profiles.

- handling house profile data, so that on the information captured by the handling house, comparison can be made between those who replied and those who did not, to detect any skews (experience shows that profiles usually match very closely indeed).

- relevant anonymised data from our extensive evaluation database.

Heinz 45

46   *Research Works*

4

WARWICK DISTRICT COUNCIL

TOWARDS AN ACTION PLAN – ACTING ON THE RESULTS OF A TENANTS' SURVEY

SUMMARY

When a large business enterprise has a turnover of approaching £40 million and employs capital assets of 10 times this amount, it would not be surprising for that company to conduct market research into how its product is received by consumers.

The results of that research would then be fed into the production process and the product – either services or goods – would be tailored to meet consumer needs and aspirations as identified. What is acceptable for private business must also be acceptable for local government – especially that part of local government, i.e. housing management, that provides a direct service to some of the most vulnerable people in society.

When Warwick District Council commissioned Market & Opinion Research International to conduct the Council's first ever piece of consumer research, the Tenant Satisfaction Survey in 1988, the members and officers were aware that the Housing Department already provided a first class housing service. Their assumptions, however, were challenged by a new Chief Housing Officer who, fired by the concept of customer care and the challenges to public sector housing by the then new legislation, persuaded the Council to test out its legitimate views by conducting independent research of the similarly legitimate views of its customers, i.e. the tenants who occupied the houses and 'enjoyed' the services offered by the Council.

In general, the results of this first survey more than confirmed the views previously held, but it accomplished something more than that. It provided an opportunity to use research not only as an input to the policy making process, but as a means of assessing the effectiveness of policy implementation.

The 1988 research undertaken by MORI revealed very high satisfaction levels among Warwick District Council tenants – in fact some of the highest found in similar studies undertaken by MORI previously. However, what was important to Warwick District Council was not those areas where the district scored well, but where the findings were less than satisfactory – indeed, there were some areas where satisfaction levels were some of the lowest found by MORI.

By analysing the data produced in the study, Warwick District Council was able to identify areas where policy initiatives were required – areas such as communications with tenants, speed and quality of repairs, efficiency of heating, consultation on proposed improvements, awareness of the legislation regarding Tenants' Choice, etc. Paternalism was, therefore, put to one side, and whilst high levels of satisfaction in terms of service delivery were recognised, it was agreed that more should be done in terms of communications and marketing and an Action Plan was therefore implemented.

The Action Plan covered special initiatives, all of which were designed to improve communications with tenants, encourage tenants to become more involved with the service they received, and to provide a more consumer/customer orientated service by way of staff training and better reception facilities. The initiatives came into being over a 16 month period, i.e. January 1989 to April 1990, and there the plan could have rested – but it did not.

It was important for the District Council to ascertain whether the initiatives had achieved their desired effects in that the service provided for tenants had not only been improved, but had been seen to improve from the tenants' point of view. Therefore, MORI was again commissioned to conduct a follow-up survey adopting exactly the same methodology, but on this occasion concentrating predominantly on those areas addressed by the initiatives adopted by the Council.

The results of the second survey went beyond the expectations of the Chief Housing Officer. The follow-up survey showed that tenants had, in the main, recognised that new initiatives had been adopted, and that these initiatives had been well received by tenants, thereby increasing previously low satisfaction rates to new heights of achievement.

As a result of the overall research initiative, Warwick District Council was able to clearly illustrate how the legitimate views and opinions of consumers can be utilised to implement change. Such research not only helps identify what changes are required, but how subsequent changes are received by those self same consumers. This particular project was not only effective in terms of measuring tenant satisfaction and opinion, it also provided positive proof that actions undertaken by the Council clearly improved the service it offered for its tenants and that tenants appreciated the improvements and were thus more likely to adopt a positive attitude to the Council should the housing service be challenged in the new competitive market.

*   *   *   *   *

TOWARDS AN ACTION PLAN
– ACTING ON THE RESULTS OF A TENANTS' SURVEY

With media reports of the financial crisis in Liverpool and the popular view of local councillors as either cloth-capped worthies or denim-clad academics, it is easy to forget that local councils are significant business enterprises and, increasingly, being run as such. It is not unusual for a local council to be the largest employer in its area and even a relatively small authority, such as Warwick District Council, has revenues in excess of £38 million p.a. and employs capital assets more than ten times this figure.

In the past, Council departments (including housing departments) were run in a professional manner – in other words, the professionals decided what services were to be provided and tenants got what they were given – and were expected to be grateful. If they didn't like it they could always go and see their local councillor, couldn't they? Services were provided *to* the consumer rather than *for* the consumer.

The 1980s, however, saw major changes in the management style and approach of local authorities. Rate-capping (and then charge-capping) put local authorities under severe financial pressure to improve their financial efficiency, and the introduction of competitive tendering (the local government equivalent of privatisation) introduced an element of the competitive market into the provision of local services. The result was an increasing interest in two concepts that the private sector has long been familiar with 'marketing' and 'customer care'. As one council employee MORI interviewed explained, "government legislation means that we have to compete with private contractors. Commercial companies have long put the customer as king – local government is slowly learning this."

Unfortunately, as a recent MORI study for the National Consumer Council showed, progress is slow. The results of the NCC study put local councils at the bottom of the league in terms of consumer satisfaction with local services – below even British Rail!

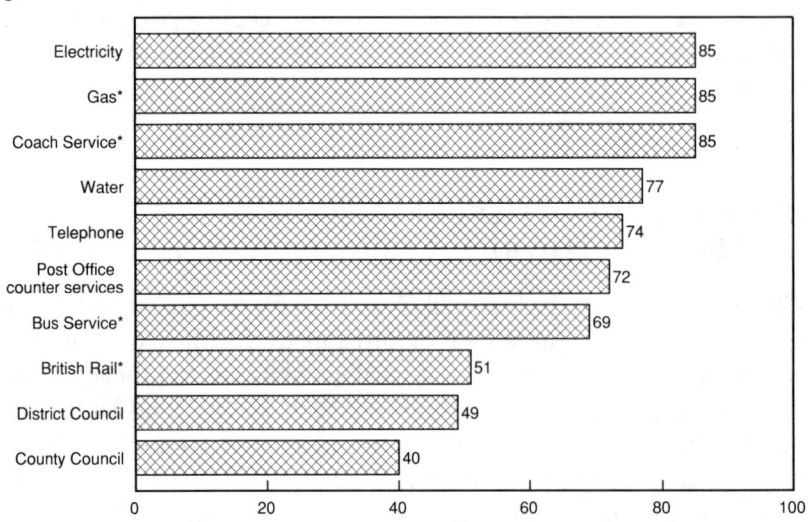

Figure 1   Satisfied with service from:

Service	%
Electricity	85
Gas*	85
Coach Service*	85
Water	77
Telephone	74
Post Office counter services	72
Bus Service*	69
British Rail*	51
District Council	49
County Council	40

Base: GB adults aged 18+
Note: * based on users
Source: MORI/NCC 1991

Nonetheless, things were changing and, as interest in marketing and customer care increased, local authorities gradually began turning to market research as an instrument to enable them to obtain a clearer understanding of the needs and wants of their 'customers' – a term often challenged in local government circles. This was certainly true in the case of Warwick District Council's Housing Department and this paper describes how the Council's Housing Officer used survey research; firstly, as an input into the policy making process and, subsequently, as a means of assessing the effectiveness of policy implementation.

Warwick District comprises the Midland towns of Warwick, Leamington Spa and Kenilworth, and the adjacent rural areas. In 1988 it was responsible for a housing stock of 7,507 properties. As is so often the case with new initiatives, the impetus for a customer survey came with the arrival of new management, in this case when the new Housing Officer joined the Council in January of that year. Although the general indications were that the Housing Department was being run in an efficient manner, he was concerned that the Department lacked reliable information on the views tenants had of the housing service and, more importantly, their requirements of the Department.

The key issues, as he saw them, were whether the housing service should be run and judged in purely economic terms, or whether the provision of customer care should be taken into consideration, and secondly, whether the service should be run on the basis of professional and political paternalism, or whether the legitimate viewpoint of tenants should be incorporated into the policy-making process. Paternalism had after all served the tenants of Warwick District Council well.

A local authority housing survey has an enormous attraction for a research agency in that it provides one of the very few occasions when researchers have the opportunity to draw a pure unclustered random sample. Warwick District Council maintains a computer database of all properties it has on its books and these were listed in geographical order and a straightforward 1 in 10 sample drawn within each of the key geographical regions used by the Housing Department. The only variation from pure random selection was a level of over-sampling in rural areas to provide a more robust sample. In all, MORI drew 1,221 names from the council list and interviewers were sent out to conduct personal in-house interviews with the individual in each household who had most dealings with the Housing Department.

The other joy of such a housing survey is the level of co-operation one achieves from respondents. People may not wish to be interviewed about some subjects, but they are keen to tell an interviewer what they think about the housing service provided by their landlord and the ways in which that service could be improved. Interviews were achieved with a total of 906 respondents – a contact rate of 74.2%. The Council was delighted with the findings of the research; initially, perhaps, due less to the value of the information provided than to the good news it brought – the tenants were quite flattering about many aspects of the housing service. Indeed, on two-thirds of the 30 measures for which MORI was able to provide comparative data, Warwick District Council received higher ratings than any other authority that MORI had previously studied. Needless to say, the new Housing Officer was pleased the members were persuaded to commission the survey!

Overall, two-thirds of tenants were satisfied with the service provided by the Housing Department and only one in five dissatisfied. What was particularly helpful to the Housing Department and members, was the context provided by the comparative data MORI was able to produce from previous surveys conducted for other councils; indeed, this was one of the major factors in awarding the contract to MORI. A 69% overall satisfaction score sounds good but it was also reassuring to know that this was the best overall rating MORI had recorded at that time.

Table 1   How satisfied are you with the service provided by .... Housing Department?

Council	Satisfied (%)
Warwick	69
Coventry	67
Richmond	61
Stevenage	58
Glasgow	56
Solihull	55
Birmingham	51
Camden	46

Base: All tenants
Source: MORI

There were also indications that Warwick Housing Department was providing a better repairs service than many other councils, and tenants were content with both the quality of the repairs and, of considerable importance, the speed with which they were carried out.

Table 2

Council	Satisfied with quality of repairs (%)	Council	Satisfied with speed of repairs (%)
Warwick	62	Warwick	56
Sutton	58	Richmond	50
Coventry	56	Coventry	48
Stevenage	55	Sutton	48
Richmond	53	Welwyn Hatfield	44
Welwyn Hatfield	53	Stevenage	40
Birmingham	45	Camden	33
Glasgow	45	Birmingham	31
Camden	42	Solihull	31
Solihull	35		

Base: All tenants
Source: MORI

But, inevitably, the results were not entirely rosy and, as is so often the case, the bad news provided some of the more actionable findings.

As we have seen, overall satisfaction with the housing repairs service was high relative to other councils, but Warwick was by no means perfect – in particular, three in ten residents were dissatisfied with the speed of repairs and a quarter were dissatisfied with the quality. In addition, there were indications of a concern about the efficiency of the heating provided in council homes. As the table below shows, Warwick was not the most highly regarded council on this issue.

Table 3   I would now like you to tell me how satisfied or dissatisfied you are with the effectiveness of the heating in your home?

Council	Satisfied(%)
Stevenage	77
Welwyn Hatfield	71
Coventry	65
Warwick	63*
Sutton	57
Richmond	49
Birmingham	49

Base: All tenants
Note: * 31% dissatisfied
Source: MORI

This concern about heating effectiveness was reflected in the type of housing improvements residents would most like to see introduced, and in the strength of their desire to see such improvements. The three most popular improvements were all linked to an improvement in heating or to insulation. Top preference was the introduction of central heating, second came replacement of windows and third came the installation of double glazing. Those who wanted to have central heating installed were the tenants who felt most strongly about their chosen improvement.

Table 4   Are there any improvements you would like the Council to carry out in your home?

	Would like (%)	Thought urgent (%)
Central heating	28	58
Replacement windows	24	54
Double glazing	13	38
New kitchen	13	30
New bathroom	10	33

Base: All tenants
Source: MORI

There were also some indications that tenants were critical of the limited influence they had had on past improvement work undertaken in their homes; 20% of those who had improvements carried out praised the Council for its consultation process, but 50% were critical.

Another slight concern highlighted in the report related to the speed of service at the Housing Office. Warwick District staff were rated highly by tenants for their friendliness, helpfulness, efficiency and interest in the customers' problems – indeed, they were the most highly rated council on each of these criteria at that date. However, tenants were somewhat more critical of the speed of service dealing with their problem, when they visited the Council offices.

Table 5   When you last contacted the Housing Office, was the person you dealt with . . . . .?

	%
Friendly	87
or unfriendly	3
Helpful	81
or unhelpful	10
Interested in your problem	67
or uninterested in your problem	16
Quick in dealing with your problem	54
or slow in dealing with your problem	31

Base: All who contacted Warwick Housing Office
Source: MORI

But tenants reserved their strongest criticism for the Council's communication activities. As we have seen, tenants were critical of the limited consultation there had been on housing improvements and the survey also revealed a broader dissatisfaction with the information provided on the Council's housing services. Only 4% of tenants believed the Council kept them fully informed, compared to 38% who believed that tenants were not told much at all about housing services.

Figure 2   How well informed do you think Warwick District Council keeps you about the services it provides?

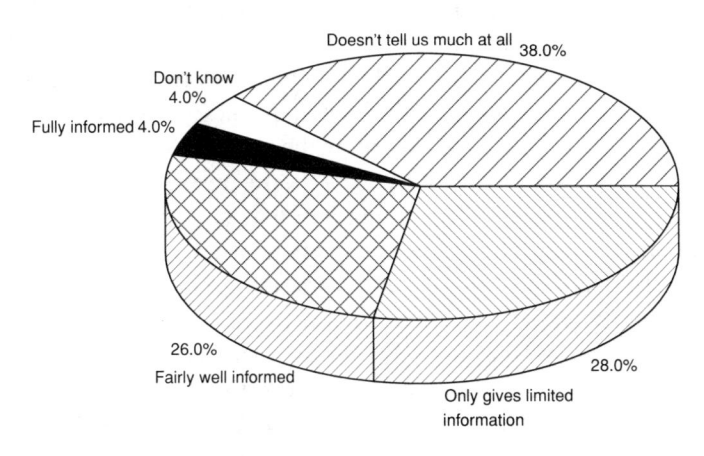

- Doesn't tell us much at all 38.0%
- Don't know 4.0%
- Fully informed 4.0%
- Fairly well informed 26.0%
- Only gives limited information 28.0%

Base: All tenants
Source: MORI

Once again, the comparative data MORI was able to provide placed these attitudes in context and showed that the criticisms made of Warwick's communications approach were not typical of all councils. On service delivery, Warwick tended to come out top; on information provision, it was one of the most poorly rated councils MORI had studied.

Table 6   How well informed do you think .... Council keeps tenants about the housing services it provides?

Council	Fully/Fairly Well Informed (%)
Welwyn Hatfield	66
Wrekin	65
Richmond	65
Birmingham	55
Camden	54
Stevenage	47
Sutton	45
York	43
Warwick	30
Glasgow	28
Solihull	27

Base: All tenants
Source: MORI

One particular area of concern for the Council was the relatively small proportion of tenants who were aware of the new government legislation concerning Tenants' Choice and the opportunity it gave to tenants to vote on the issue of transferring ownership of their homes away from the Council. On the one hand, it was reassuring to the Council that 80% of tenants would prefer their homes to continue to be owned by the Council, but officers and members were disappointed that only 22% were aware of the voting provision contained in the new legislation and that only 54% of tenants would be certain to vote. The introduction of this new legislation had provided some of the impetus for the survey and the Council had intended to use the results to help plan its response.

The results of the study were presented to the members of the Council and MORI used a particular presentational trick to highlight the value of the research findings. Before the results were fully available, MORI selected a number of questions from the survey and sent a form containing these questions to all members and senior officers. Recipients of the form were asked to estimate what they expected tenants' answers to be to the chosen questions. The forms were collected and the final results were presented in parallel to members' and officers' 'guesstimates'. The effect was to highlight areas where there were significant differences between the expected views of tenants and their actual views.

Although there were some individual surprises, the findings of the research drew a picture of the Council's Housing Services that was very much in line with the Housing Officer's expectations when he first suggested conducting a survey. The Department did operate in a professional manner, and did deliver a satisfactory quality of service to its customers. However, it was clearly paternalistic in its approach and did little to market its services to tenants, inform them of which services it could provide, or consult them on changes that would affect them.

The Council decided that some of the key findings of the study should be acted upon and, following considerable internal discussions of the report findings, the research led directly to a series of action points devised by the Housing Department. This action plan comprised the following key elements:

1) The introduction of a Repairs (Dis)Satisfaction Card in order to monitor the repairs service. It will be recalled that although satisfaction was high relative to other councils, this was partly due to their poor performance, and that a significant proportion of Warwick tenants were unhappy with the speed and quality of the repairs service.

2) A series of meetings were to be arranged on 'Tenants' Choice'. This was in response to the low level of awareness of the implications of the 1988 Housing Act.

3) The concept that tenants should be consulted on, and offered a choice of, improvement, was to be pursued. Tenants had expressed concern about the lack of consultation and this tied in with more general concern about the limited quantity of information provided by the Council.

4) A new budget to cover marketing of the Department and the creation of a Tenants' Handbook and Newsletter. This was in response to the highly critical report on tenant's attitude toward council communications.

5) The recruitment of an additional receptionist in the Housing Office and the refurbishment of the waiting areas. This was in response to concerns about the speed with which enquiries were being handled at the Housing Office.

6) An increase in the Department training budget by 300%. This was not in direct response to survey recommendations, but was tied in with concerns about communications and customer care.

7) A rolling programme to improve lighting on estates to enhance security. This was not actually a recommendation from the survey; tenants were generally satisfied with security and lighting, but the Housing Department's professional viewpoint was that levels of dissatisfaction were, nevertheless, unacceptable.

The issues of heating and insulation were not addressed by the Action Plan as the Council had already initiated a programme of improvements in these areas. All recommendations were accepted and members made no other suggestions for action.

As a direct result of the research and the subsequent Action Plan, the following activities were undertaken:

1) A Tenancy Conditions Review	–	January 1989
2) Adoption of a Formal Consultation Policy	–	August 1989
3) Customer Care Awareness Training	–	Autumn 1989
4) 20 Tenants' meetings	–	Autumn 1989
5) Information and Marketing Budget	–	November 1989
6) Repair Satisfaction Cards introduced	–	early 1990
7) Tenants' Handbook launched	–	April 1990
8) Tenants' Newsletter launched	–	April 1990

That could have been that. The research had been undertaken, the results analysed, an action plan drawn up, and the action plan implemented. But that was not sufficient for the Council's Housing Officer, he wanted to know how tenants had reacted to the changes and he wanted to examine the reaction to a number of other proposals. Consequently, he obtained Council permission to repeat the study in September 1990, two years on.

The second survey was undertaken in exactly the same manner as the first survey and this time MORI achieved a contact rate of 72.8%. The results, in some respects were a replication of the findings of the 1988 study; Warwick District Council was still highly regarded by its tenants in terms of its service delivery (though it had lost its pre-eminent position to Lincoln City Council). However, some of the shifts in response enabled the Council's Housing Department to judge the impact of its initiatives and, encouragingly, they seemed to have had a significant impact.

Firstly, the Council's original programme for the installation of central heating had borne fruit. Satisfaction with the effectiveness of heating in tenants' homes increased sharply, with the proportion *very* satisfied increasing dramatically from 40% to 61%. This was probably one reason for the increase in the proportion of tenants who were very satisfied with the value for money they received for the rents they paid (up from 28% to 38%).

The Repairs Satisfaction Card, which had been introduced six months earlier, appeared to have had some impact; 48% of those who had had a repair completed recalled having received a card, and 42% of this group had returned the card. Most made favourable comments, but the survey provided the council with the reassurance that they were not merely hearing from satisfied customers – those who told MORI that they were unhappy with their repairs were as likely (in fact marginally more likely) to return a card than those who were satisfied with the quality of the repair. In fact the Council was only seeking information from dissatisfied tenants.

The tenants' meetings that the Council initiated to communicate the issues surrounding Tenants' Choice appeared to have had an impact, though this was somewhat limited. Awareness of tenants' right to vote on housing transfer had increased (from 22% to 32%), but the proportion who intended to vote had not altered significantly.

The increase in staffing at the Housing Office, and the training that had been introduced in customer care, seemed to have had some impact on tenants' experiences at the Housing Office. There had been no significant shift in perception of the friendliness, helpfulness, or interest of staff (these were already high), but there was a significant increase in the proportion of visitors who felt that their problem had been handled promptly.

Table 7   When you last contacted .... Housing Office, was the person you dealt with?

	1988	1990	
	%	%	%
Friendly	87	89	+2
Helpful	81	84	+3
Interested in your problem	67	72	+5
Quick in dealing with your problem	54	64	+10

Base: All contacting Housing Office
Source: MORI

The indications were that the customer care programme had impacted on tenants' views of the Council but the big (and welcome) surprise of the second survey was the impact of the Department's activities in the field of marketing.

Figure 3   Which of the phrases on this card best describes the extent to which you have looked at ....?

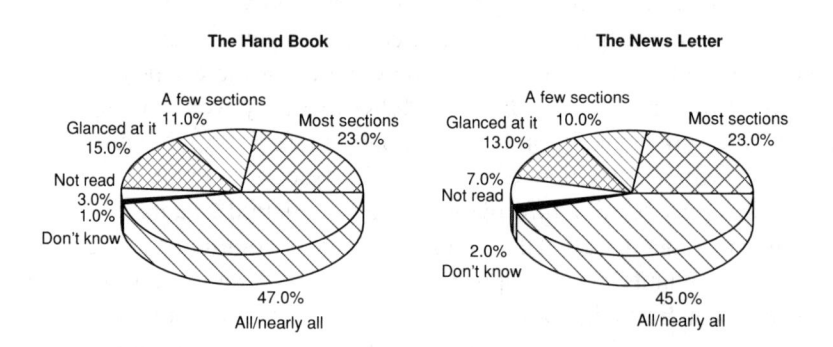

The Hand Book
- A few sections 11.0%
- Most sections 23.0%
- Glanced at it 15.0%
- Not read 3.0%
- Don't know 1.0%
- All/nearly all 47.0%

The News Letter
- A few sections 10.0%
- Most sections 23.0%
- Glanced at it 13.0%
- Not read 7.0%
- Don't know 2.0%
- All/nearly all 45.0%

Base: All tenants having received each
Source: MORI

It will be recalled that in April 1990, the Housing Department had introduced a Tenants' Handbook and a Tenants' Newsletter. The former was a compendium of information for tenants on the services the council provided, contact points and procedures. The Newsletter provided information on topical issues relating to tenants, tenants' associations and housing in general in the district.

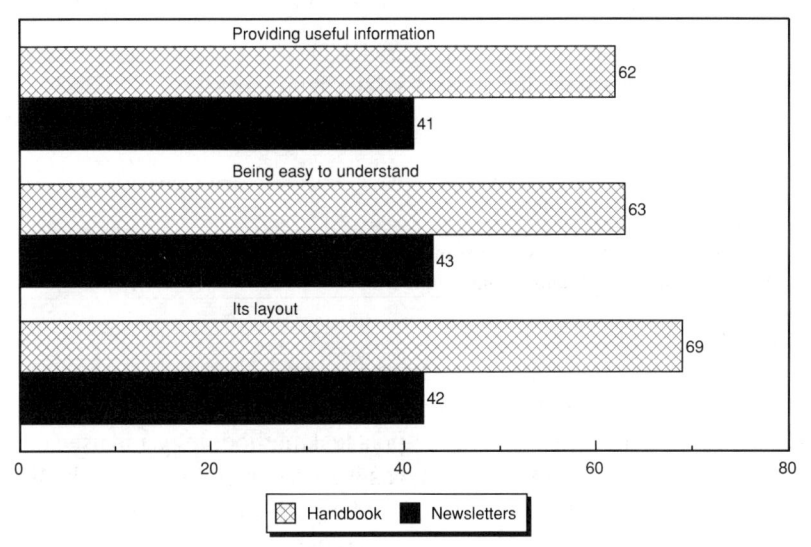

Figure 4   How would you rate .... in terms ....?
Percentage answering "Very good."

	Handbook	Newsletters
Providing useful information	62	41
Being easy to understand	63	43
Its layout	69	42

Base: All tenants having received each
Source: MORI

Tenants interviewed were well aware of both these publications; 75% remembered receiving a copy of the Newsletter (73% had received the most recent issue) and 88% had received a copy of the Tenants' Handbook. Encouragingly, 95% of those who had received the handbook still had a copy.

It was also clear that these publications were being read; nearly half claimed to have read all or nearly all of each and hardly anyone said that they had not looked at them.

Both publications were well regarded in terms of the usefulness of the information they contained, their ease of comprehension and their layout.

The greatest impact of the Action Plan was, however, on tenants' sense of being kept informed. It will be recalled that, in 1988, Warwick was poorly regarded in this respect in comparison with other councils, and only 30% of tenants felt they were kept at least fairly well informed about the housing services the Council provided. In 1988, Warwick had been the second most poorly regarded, in terms of the information that it provided to tenants, of all the councils MORI had studied in the previous two years. In 1990, all this changed and Warwick was shown to be the most highly regarded council MORI had studied in two years. The proportion who felt the Council kept them at least fairly well informed more than doubled from 30% to 61%.

Table 8   How well do you think Warwick District Council keeps tenants about the housing service it provides?

	1988 %	1990 %	% Change
Keeps us fully informed	4	11	+7
Keeps us fairly well informed	26	50	+24
Gives us only a limited amount of information	28	21	-7
Doesn't tell us much at all about what's going on	38	14	-24

Base: All tenants
Source: MORI

The research programme undertaken by MORI was not an intricate programme. It relied on a classic pre-post test methodology and used classic random sampling techniques, but it was well received by Warwick District Council (and not only because the results painted the Council in a good light). The research worked because the Housing Officer had a clear idea of what he wished to find out from the survey, the skills to translate the findings into an Action Plan, and the ability to have that Plan approved by the Council. The research proved particularly effective because MORI was able to focus on the key issues highlighted by the Housing Department and because the results were clearly communicated to decisions-makers in the Council. The ability of the research to set Warwick in the 'competitive' environment, and position its image in relation to that of other councils, enhanced members' and officers' understanding of the significance of the findings. The project demonstrated that effectiveness need not be synonymous with complexity, and that rigorous research techniques, combined with an understanding of the market being surveyed and clear guidance from the client, will result in cost-effective, actionable research.

5

THAMES TELEVISION

EFFECTIVELY RESEARCHING THE BUSINESS COMMUNITY

SUMMARY

Motivation

With the exception of those legally prohibited, any provider of goods or services may take advantage of the power of television to reach their customers. Business Development within the television environment must constantly look beyond the existing customer base and develop entirely original areas of advertising to the medium.

At Thames the commitment to developing these new areas for our medium is a central plank in our Business Development strategy. New research initiatives must therefore not only persuade clients of the power of television, but further the relevance of weekday television. In short, they will help maximise airtime revenue potential for the station.

Having identified London's clear importance to advertisers wishing to address business people, it was necessary to commission research to demonstrate the effectiveness of TV in reaching this target audience over the more conventionally used quality press. These advertisers should also be shown that weekday television was at least equally effective as weekend in the London region. To do this we needed to demonstrate that conventional proxies for the viewing of business people, ABC1 or AB men viewing figures from BARB, were not necessarily a reliable base for planning decisions.

The Chosen Route

BMRB was approached to provide a means of measuring the media consumption of business people in the London ITV region cost effectively. An ability to discriminate between different types of business people with flexible analysis in-house and swift turn-arounds were stipulated. BMRB identified the AB TGI, a sample of AB heads of household where detailed information relating to consumption of products and services has already been collected. Critically for our survey, detailed information on the occupations of respondent and spouse are also collected, allowing an identification of a genuine sample of business people.

Out of nearly 1,000 contacted, 675 were eligible and we hoped that 60% would complete four weeks of media diaries, measuring quarter-hour television viewing and radio listening along with readership of national newspapers, the principal local newspapers and listings magazines.

In the end 57% or 384 business people completed the four weekly media diaries having initially provided additional information on their specific function in the decision-making process for various business products. Viewing to all channels was collected including satellite and cable where available, video viewing and detailed radio consumption by station. Press patronage and cinema going were also collected.

The Findings

The survey clearly met our principal objective of showing the strength of Thames ITV in reaching the broad group of business people. Over 75% watched Thames ITV at some stage in an average week and on Channel 4, Thames-time patronage was over 40%. These relatively high figures, which in each case were higher than those for London Weekend Television, rebut two common misnomers, namely that business people never watch television, or that if they do it is only at the weekend.

The single source nature of the survey allowed direct comparison with other media. Two of the most recognised vehicles for reaching business people, the *Financial Times* and *Times* reach only 20% of business people in an average week on the basis of accumulated readership over six days.

Numerically the most successful radio station, Capital FM, reached little more than one quarter of business people in a week, with LBC at only one in eight.

The absolute amount of commercial television viewing, although relatively light at 5½ hours per week, was clearly identifiable and predictable from the survey, another key objective in refuting the argument that this group was impossible to target using television.

All this was gratifying in itself but Thames wished to target potential advertisers about *real groups* of business people, such as decision makers on relocation and business air travellers. Provision of the data by BMRB on their CHOICES PC-based desktop system allowed literally hundreds of different discriminators to be examined in the business arena, with relative ease, against any or all of the media consumption parameters. It also allowed examples of coverage of these varied business groups, against real or constructed campaign schedules, to be considered.

Fine tuning of these schedules, using detailed information of the viewing preferences of the specific business people groupings, have allowed advertisers to plan campaigns which maximise efficiency and reduce apparent wastage. The removal of another canard, the 'scattergun' nature of television in comparison with some quality press, is a direct result with many clients.

The Result

Much has been achieved in the six months that the survey has been used, although given the scope of the information, much potential still exists for further work.

A direct result has been new business wins comfortably paying for this research, the clearest example being a very substantial London campaign booked by Alliance International on behalf of Apricot Computers, greatly aided by the survey findings, and importantly, solely utilising Thames airtime.

This research has clearly shown the strength of television, particularly Thames Television, in targeting and effectively reaching the business community.

* * * * *

BACKGROUND

The data requirements of a television contractor are broad indeed. "Every commercial you've ever seen" is just a starting point. Any station paying more than lip-service to Business Development will also need information on categories that are not on television – yet could be.

At Thames the commitment to Business Development is unequivocal. It is regarded as the life-blood of the sales drive. The icing on the agency sales cake. It is not so long ago that there was no financial advertising on television – now it is a major category for the medium at large. The search for new advertising areas, for Thames in particular, must go on.

It should also be remembered that the London television marketplace is different. Forget satellite, cable and the 'new' developments, television in London is already highly competitive. It is quite possible for the Business Development unit of one of the London stations to 'win' a client onto television – and then lose the business to the other. As a consequence, any information that adds value to, in our case, the weekday proposition has great potential worth.

With these thoughts in mind, a decision was made to invest some of our 1990 ad hoc research budget into a project that would attempt to gain television, and more importantly Thames Television, an edge in a sector until recently regarded as largely the province of the quality press – that of advertising which targets business people.

We knew that the claim of London, the ITV region, was strong. Marginally less than 20% of UK households, but 28% of shareholders, 32% of higher turnover companies (£5m +), 42% of businessmen, from the BMRC definition (see Appendix 1), 45% of the top 10,000 companies and almost half of the fastest-growing companies, yet many agencies wanted to drag the conversation back to where they felt most comfortable – 26% of ABC1 men.

Specifically we wanted to try to get away from this automatic 'funnelling' of any business proposition that we initiated into the nearest convenient BARB category. We found that agencies and advertisers had become conditioned largely by what was available from the accepted industry research source.

It seemed not to matter if the product or service to be promoted was an airline, a computer, a relocation proposition or even a courier service – the target referred to was 'businessmen' and the accepted BARB surrogate almost always ABC1 men.

We set out, with BMRB, to investigate ways of producing a sample of business people, (yes 'people' not just men) which would be of sufficient size to allow detailed sub-group analysis. We wanted to look, for instance, at those business people who had flown abroad on business within the last 12 months. We wanted to look at their viewing, not just of ITV and

Channel 4 but also of BBC1 and BBC2. And of their satellite station viewing. And their viewing of video material.

We also mentioned to BMRB that we wanted full details of their exposure to commercial radio. And daily readership patterns. And frequency of cinema visits. By about 500 discriminators!

FINDINGS

Patronage

When confronted with a group of 'business people', face to face, the same comment recurs with some frequency, "Of course I'm no use to you as I don't watch television." Our first objective, simply at a level of total business people, was to challenge this particular stance. The findings, happily, were encouraging.

Over 75% of our total sample of 384 watched Thames ITV at some stage during an average week. On Channel 4, Thames-time patronage was a little over 40%. These figures were high in absolute terms and in each case higher than the London Weekend Television equivalent. So far, so good.

The single source nature of the research meant that we could compare these patronage results with other media. Expressed as Average Issue Readership we found that the *Daily Mail* (20%), *Daily Telegraph* (17%) and *Evening Standard* (15%) were the most successful daily newspapers in reaching the London business community.

By giving the leading titles six days to accumulate readership, results built as follows:

Table 1

Daily Mail	29%
Daily Telegraph	28%
Evening Standard (5 days)	23%
The Times	20%
Financial Times	20%
The Independent	17%

Commercial radio was another medium whose efficiency in reaching business people we wanted to check. Expressed as Weekly Patronage, findings were as follows overleaf:

Table 2

Capital FM	26%
Capital Gold	15%
LBC FM	12%
LBC Talkback	4%
All Others	19%

The patronage argument, therefore, proved not too hard to overcome. The apparent oddity, at the head of these rankings, of a newspaper and a radio station not renowned for business advertising did not surprise us. Indeed, we anticipated *Coronation Street* being probably the top-rated ITV programme for business people. The sheer volume of audience achieved by the most popular programmes usually guarantees success across all demographics.

Hours of Viewing

The next perceived wisdom that we needed to challenge was that of Hours of Viewing. This one was much harder to counter. "If I do watch any commercial television, then it's so little that an advertiser would never know where to reach me" goes the standard argument and they do have a point.

We found the viewing of commercial television by business people to be light, at around 5½ hours/week on average, but predictable, to a greater degree than almost all other demographics, at least during the week.

Key Programmes

The single key programme for business people in London is, without doubt, the *Nine O'Clock News* on BBC1. However, the audience falls away so sharply on BBC1 from 21:30 onwards that TV Ratings for the News of around 25, regularly drop well into single figures for the following programme. This, coupled with the successful performance of *News at Ten* and the programmes immediately around it, was very much what we were hoping to find. The 1991 Thames business proposition was beginning to take shape.

TV ratings for business people, of around 15, were fairly easy to find on Thames and these, when added to the specific targeting opportunities, offered by post 22:30 programmes such as *The City Programme, 01, Midweek Sports Special* and quality feature films were to form the bedrock of many of our proposed business schedules.

The weekend picture, although of less actionable relevance to ourselves, was nevertheless interesting. The selectivity of programme choice amongst business people was particularly clearly demonstrated on Sundays where reasonable amounts of viewing could be found as early as lunchtime with Brian Walden, during the afternoon with football highlights in *The London Match* and on into peak-time. Interestingly, the flagship arts programme, *The South Bank Show* achieved very low ratings amongst business people.

So, just as during the week, this particular group demonstrated a propensity for viewing specific programmes and then either switching the set off or tuning to another channel when their chosen programme had finished. They proved to be as anticipated, light viewers, but also, encouragingly, highly selective viewers.

Viewing Patterns

One of the key reasons for commissioning the research, as stated earlier, was to check on the validity of using ABC1 men from BARB as a surrogate category for business people. Consequently, a comparison was made between the two data sets, expressed as quarter-hour TVRs, averaged individually across the full four weeks within each of the seven days. Once again the results were pleasing, because although overall viewing levels were similar, within specific days there were significant differences (see Figures 1 - 7 in Appendix 3).

From Monday through to Friday we found a similar relationship between ABC1 men viewing from BARB and business people viewing from this survey. On each day business people viewed ITV at a lower level than ABC1 men prior to 19:30, reflecting a reduced availability to view at that time. However, their viewing for selected programmes after that time, including *The Bill*, *The Match*, *LA Law*, *Capital City* and *News at Ten* was well above the level of ABC1 men, as recorded by BARB.

The weekend pattern of viewing was obviously very different, with Saturday performing quite strongly against the BARB equivalent, whilst Sunday was the poorest day of the week in comparative terms.

Sub Groups

As stated previously, the primary intended function of the research was as an aid to business development for Thames. We wanted to talk to advertisers – both existing and potential – about the actual people they wanted to reach. To address this issue we began to look at the data on a sub-category level.

Within the database of 384 business people, BMRB provided a full check on sample strength for all available AB TGI cross-tabs, as well as those within the additional questionnaire. Without considering any sub-groups generating samples of less than around 70, many hundreds of discriminators became available for detailed multi-media analysis.

The following list details examples of a few of these possibilities, together with the sample:

Table 3

Business people	Sample
who pay for business lunches with a personal credit card.	133
who have or own a home computer	160
who made international calls from home in the last year	107
who have lived in their current home for less than four years	161
with 2 or more cars in the household	216
who work in financial services	116
who play golf	87
who are involved in the final decision on the purchase of office systems	141

For each of the full range of discriminators, such as those illustrated here, we were able to measure press patronage, exposure to radio and frequency of cinema visits, as well as the same degree of television analysis that was carried out against the whole sample.

It is obviously difficult to generalise findings from such a vast range of sub-groups, but it is worth pointing out a constant trend, whereby the more senior the analysed group, the more selective their media consumption became. For example, analysis of directors and the most senior managers in financial companies revealed a drop in average weekly hours viewed (of commercial television) from 5.4 for all business people to 4.8.

However, this served only to increase the predictability of their viewing by showing proportionally more of it to be conducted post 21:30. It also, encouragingly for us, demonstrated a widening gap in patronage levels between Thames (79%) and London Weekend (68%).

EFFECTIVE SELLING

Coverage and Frequency

During October 1990 there were a number of television campaigns running in London, targeting elements of the business community. We took one of these, for Compaq Computers, and made a comparison of campaign achievement as measured by, firstly, the accepted BARB surrogate grouping, secondly, total business people from this survey and finally the key sub-group required by the advertiser – those business people involved in the decision making process on the purchase of office systems.

Findings were as follows:

Table 4

	BARB ABC1 Men	Business People	Decision Makers Office Systems
TV Ratings	355	363	367
1 + Coverage	81	87	87
Average Frequency	4.4	4.2	4.2

Thus the use of the surrogate BARB category, in this case ABC1 men, proved a good guide to total rating levels, although the coverage and frequency make-up was slightly different.

Proposal

The availability of coverage and frequency facilities has proved invaluable from a business development viewpoint. We have been able to construct dummy October schedules, show them to potential advertisers and demonstrate their likely achievement against their aspirational target groups, maximising efficiency and reducing apparent wastage.

Detailed below is part of a Thames proposal to a current 'press-only' advertiser:

Table 5

	BARB ABC1 Men	Business People	Decision Makers Office Systems
TV Ratings	300	326	358
1 + Coverage	77	78	80
Average Frequency	3.9	4.1	4.4

By using the data in this way it has helped greatly in allaying oft-repeated advertiser fears about the perceived 'scattergun' approach of commercial television, particularly in comparison with certain elements of the Quality Press.

Conclusions

The scale and scope of this research project is vast. We have now worked the database extensively for six months and have still only scratched the surface of all that could be done. However, much has been achieved already.

The realism of our approach in readily acknowledging the wisdom of a mixed-media approach to business targeting has been widely applauded, whilst our efforts to quantify the strength of each of the component parts have been met positively by our existing client base.

Perception of Thames as a commissioner and objective interpreter of quality research has been enhanced, amongst both advertisers and agencies.

And finally, yes, we have already won business by using this research. It has comfortably paid for itself. Confidentiality precludes me from naming advertisers who will be using Thames to achieve their business targeting objectives later this year. However, a very substantial London television campaign, booked by Alliance International on behalf of Apricot Computers, has solely utilised Thames airtime, with a schedule greatly influenced by the findings of this study.

The research has helped prove that television in general, and Thames Television in particular, has a major role to play in targeting the business community.

METHODOLOGY

The Sample

The target sample was defined as AB business men and women living in the London ITV Region. A full list of eligible occupations was selected by Thames Television and is detailed in Appendix 2.

In order to obtain the sample cost effectively, it was decided to use BMRB's AB TGI database. AB TGI is a sample of AB heads of household and/or housewives who have completed a detailed questionnaire on their use of products, services and media. The initial contact vehicle is a national telephone omnibus survey of all adults. During that interview, respondents who are identified as AB heads of household/housewives are invited to take part in a further survey. Those who agree are sent an AB TGI questionnaire. The response rates for the 1989 and 1990 surveys were as follows:

Table 6

	1989		1990	
AB HoH/HW identified	8,956	100%	9,376	100%
Refused further survey	1,490	17%	1,958	21%
Sent Questionnaire	7,466	83%	7,418	79%
Returned usable questionnaire	5,520	62%	5,514	59%

The returned questionnaires contained detailed information on the occupations both of the respondent and, where appropriate, the spouse/partner. This meant that it was possible to select either the original respondent or the spouse/partner on the basis of an eligible occupation. (In a small number of cases, both would have been eligible for selection. Where this occurred, the original respondent was selected).

It was our aim to finish with a final sample of circa 400 who had kept a media diary for four weeks. Allowing for initial refusals, failure to stay the course, diaries lost in post, we had hoped we would get a 60% success rate. At the time of sampling, we had full data from the 1989 AB TGI and January-June 1990 AB TGI. These yielded 582 eligible respondents – 'business people' in the London ITV area – plus a further 382 'spouses'. However, it was unlikely that all of these would qualify for inclusion in the final sample. Some were bound to have moved. Others, although in the London ITV area, would be unable to receive the London station.

Data Collection

The survey was conducted in two stages:

(i) Recruitment Stage – conducted via a telephone interview.

(ii) Main data collection – via completion of four weekly media diaries.

Recruitment Stage

The 964 persons identified from the AB TGI samples were re-contacted by telephone. At this stage, eligibility was checked by ensuring that the respondent was still employed in the qualifying occupation and lived in a household which received Thames TV. In the event, 30% were found to be ineligible – a small proportion could not be contacted at all, others had moved away, changed occupation or could not receive Thames TV.

Table 7

	Total		AB TGI Respondents		Partners of AB TGI Respondents	
All names identified as eligible on AB TGI	964	100%	582	100%	382	100%
Moved/died	51	5%	36	6%	15	4%
Telephone number unobtainable	43	4%	27	5%	16	4%
Ineligible – changed profession	67	7%	49	8%	18	5%
Ineligible – does not receive London ITV	128	13%	78	13%	50	13%
All eligible sample	675	70%	392	67%	283	74%

We attempted to recruit eligible respondents to keep a four week diary. Additional data on specific business products were collected at this stage. It was also necessary to ask the 'partners' to complete an AB TGI questionnaire. The field work for the recruitment stage took place between 13th-26th September 1990. All interviews were conducted by fully trained members of BMRB's specialist telephone unit – TMRB. The data collection and sample management were administered by CATI (Computer Assisted Telephone Interview) system.

The Diaries

Following the initial recruitment stage, eligible respondents were sent a self completion diary for four consecutive weeks. The diary was designed as a short term media study and covered the period Monday 1st to Sunday 28th October 1990.

Data were recorded, day by day, quarter-hour by quarter-hour from 06:30 to 02:00 for:

Table 8

Viewing to :	Listening to :
BBC1	BBC National (1,2,3,4,5)
BBC2	BBC Local
ITV	Capital FM
C4	Capital Gold
Satellite/Cable	LBC Crown
Hired/bought video	LBC
Self recorded video	Jazz FM
	Melody
	Other commercial

In addition, for each day of the week, respondents were asked to record which of 13 daily, 11 Sunday newspapers and 2 programme magazines they had read that day and whether they had been to the cinema.

To encourage participation, respondents were offered incentives. These took the form of gift vouchers and the face value for each of the first three weeks was the same, but a bonus voucher was offered for the final week. Since respondents were informed of the terms in advance, it was thought that this would encourage continuous co-operation.

In addition, respondents were telephoned each week to deal with any problems they might have had and to remind them to return each diary when it was completed.

In the event, our initial estimates of responses were justified:

Table 9

Eligible Sample	675	100%
Unable to contact specific respondent	131	19%
Respondent refused interview	84	12%
Respondent agreed to interview but refused to keep diary	33	5%
Agreed to keep diary	427	63%
Refused survey after initial agreement	19	3%
Not all documents returned/useable	24	4%
All diaries returned and usable	384	57%

Although over 400 respondents did return some diaries, it was not appropriate to extend the sample beyond those who had completed the full four weeks – including a small number who had been on holiday in weeks 2 and/or 3, but who had informed us of this and who were at home during the first and fourth weeks – since it was important to be able to provide data on cumulative reach over four weeks.

DATA ANALYSIS

The Data Analysis System

It was of prime importance that the analysis system should be easy to use, in-house, and give quick responses to the demands to be made on it by the sales department. Thames TV had carefully considered the range of analyses which would be required to satisfy their needs. Although primarily interested in TV data, it was also important to see to what extent other media – radio and press in particular – might give additional cover and/or frequency.

They had therefore specified a series of different requirements which can best be summarised as follows:

(a) Quarter-hour ratings.

(b) Net reach for any group of quarter-hour segments.

(c) Weekly and four weekly reach for specified time segments, day by day, weekday, weekend and all week.

(d) Average hours of viewing/listening for the same time segments as in (c) above.

(e) Derived from (a) and (d) would be share of viewing/listening for individual quarter-hours or time segments.

All of these were required for the four terrestrial channels, but total viewing was defined in three ways:

(i) The sum of the four terrestrial channels

(ii) As (i) but including cable/satellite

(iii) As (ii) but including VCR viewing

Similarly, data were required for each of the commercial radio stations, the total to include BBC.

To facilitate ease of data recovery, we decided to use our PC-based software – CHOICES. This is a menu-driven system, all card/column/punches being compiled in a dictionary such that, by following an English language series of questions on screen, a list of English language answers are shown and the user selects those required for the analysis. As well as all the data from the diaries, the answers from the AB TGI questionnaire were loaded into the system. This was to allow any of the analysis detailed above to be filtered through any single target or combination of targets.

CHOICES has the facility to quickly process cross tabulations of individual or logic (and, or, not) statements. It can also provide volumetric – and, therefore, average data – provided that values have been attached to responses. While it would have been possible to attach values to all the quarter-hour codes individually, this would have significantly increased the size of the dictionary and that increase, combined with the necessity to undertake a large number of computations to arrive at the results listed above, would have slowed the response unacceptably. It was therefore necessary to undertake a large scale preparation of the database before it was loaded into the system.

Data Preparation

The individual weeks covered by the diary period were not, in themselves, important. The results were to be used to demonstrate what would occur in an average week, or over a four week period.

To exemplify this, Thames TV might wish to show what the average weekly reach would be for a Monday on Channel 4 between 17:15 and 20:00 hours. There were four sets of data from four weeks to answer this. Providing a net figure for each week was simple. To provide the average entailed treating each net figure as part of a volumetric analysis with a weight of 0.25 such that the addition of the four weighted weeks would provide the average.

Similarly, to calculate the average homes viewing of Channel 4 in that time period meant adding together all the quarter-hours and coding each respondent – on several columns – such that the unit value was 0.0625 (0.25 per quarter-hour x 0.25 for one week out of four), there was 0.1875 (3 x 0.0625) the 10's value was 0.625 etc.

These summary codes were provided for each TV channel, each radio station – for each designated time segment – for each day of the week – Thames week-versus-LWT week – all week etc.

This summary coding ensured that the calculation time on CHOICES was a matter of seconds, enabling the sales personnel to respond to questions with the minimum amount of delay.

APPENDICES

Appendix 1

Definition of a BMRC Businessman

The descriptive definition of a BMRC businessman is :

> "A man or woman whose occupation implies the exercise of significant managerial, executive, technical or advisory functions and who works in an organisation eligible on grounds of size".

In practice eligibility depends on satisfying a number of detailed criteria:

1. That the informant has managerial responsibilities or has qualifications of degree standard which are relevant to his occupation.

2. That with the exception of a small number of technically qualified C1s meeting criterion 1, the informant would be classified as A or B social grade.

3. That the size of the establishment in which the informant works satisfies the following minimum size conditions

retail, wholesale, construction	– 25 employees
industrial and financial services	– 10 employees
professional and consultancy services	– no minimum

4. That the informant's occupation is eligible.

Appendix 2

List of Occupations – From AB TGI Survey

All working full time in occupation:

Accountant

Finance, investment, insurance and tax specialist

Architect/town planner

Quantity surveyor (and at least one person reports directly to them)

Building, land and mining surveyor (with at least one person reporting directly to them)

Industrial designer

Draughtsmen (with at least 5 people reporting directly to them)

Economist/statistician/actuary

Systems analyst/computer programmer (with responsibility for at least 5 people)

Chemical engineer – qualified (and responsible for at least 10 people)

Mechanical engineer – qualified (and responsible for at least 10 people)

Mining quarry engineer – qualified (and responsible for at least 10 people)

Technical engineer – qualified (and responsible for a least 10 people)

Marketing/sales manager/executive market research manager/executive

Advertising/PR manager/executive

Bank manager (and responsible for at least 4 people)

Construction manager (and responsible for at least 20 people)

Food /drink/tobacco manager (and responsible for at least 20 people)

Food/drink retail or wholesale (and responsible for at least 50 people)

Textile manufacture manager (and responsible for at least 20 people)

Footwear manufacture manager (and responsible for at least 20 people)

Paper manufacture manager (and responsible for at least 20 people)

Rubber/metal manufacturing manager (and responsible for at least 20 people)

Metal goods/vehicle manager (and responsible for at least 20 people)

Printing/publishing manager (and responsible for at least 5 people)

Timber/wooden furniture manager (and responsible for at least 20 people)

Transport, air, rail, sea/harbour manager (and responsible for at least 20 people)

Mining/public utilities, water, gas, electricity manager (and responsible for at least 20 people)

National government – HEO, LEO, SEO, Assistant Principal (and responsible for at least 50 people)

Local government – chief officer, director

Local government – assistant, deputy officer, director

Judges/lawyers/solicitors (and responsible for at least 20 people)

Company secretary/trade union secretary/charities secretary/legal secretary (and responsible for at least 20 people)

Appendix 3 – ITV Quarter-Hour Viewing: Average All Business People

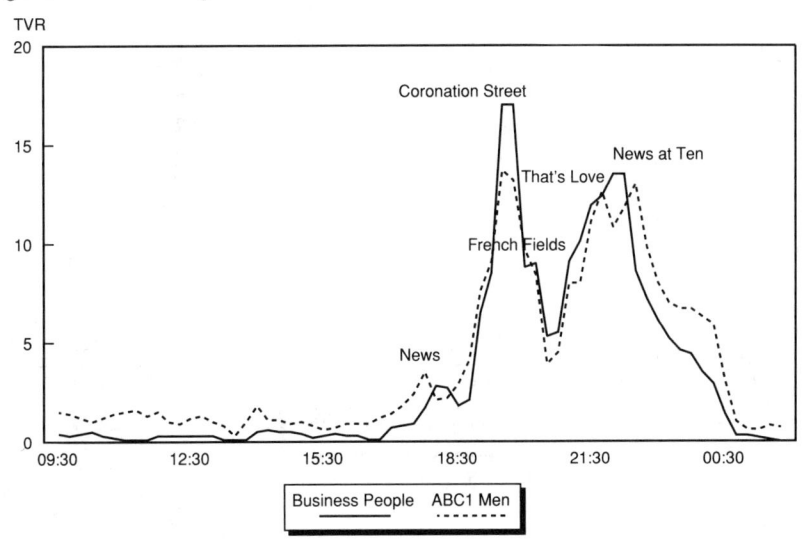

Figure 1   Monday

Figure 2   Tuesday

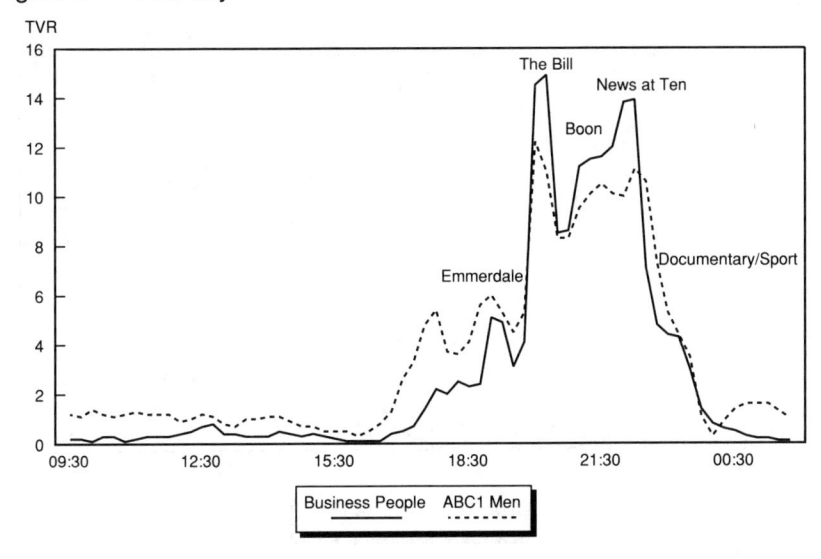

82 Research Works

Figure 3   Wednesday

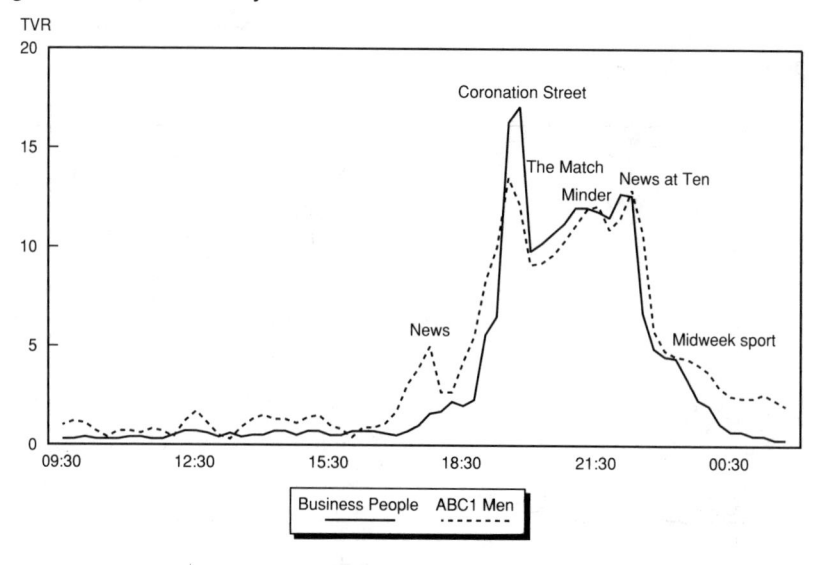

Business People / ABC1 Men viewing on Wednesday, showing peaks at News, Coronation Street, The Match, Minder, News at Ten, and Midweek sport.

Figure 4   Thursday

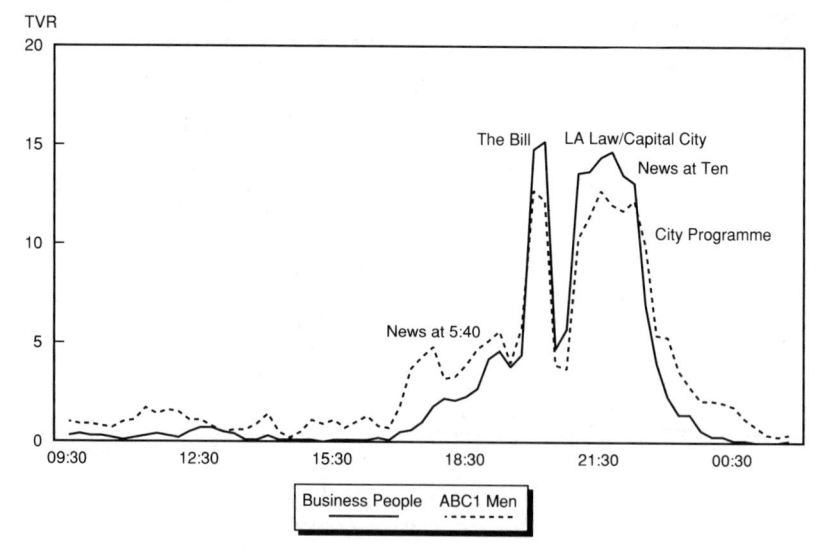

Business People / ABC1 Men viewing on Thursday, showing peaks at News at 5:40, The Bill, LA Law/Capital City, News at Ten, and City Programme.

Figure 5 Friday

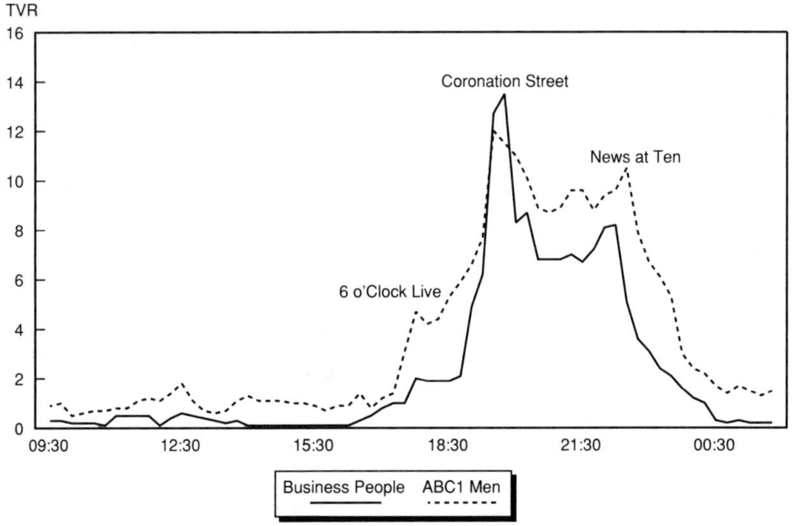
TVR
16
14
12
10
8
6
4
2
0
Coronation Street
News at Ten
6 o'Clock Live
09:30
12:30
15:30
18:30
21:30
00:30
Business People
ABC1 Men

Figure 6 Saturday

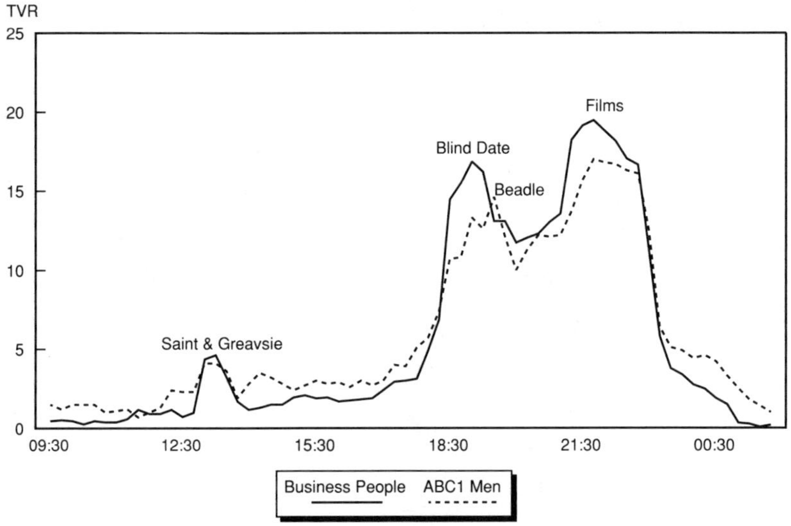
TVR
25
20
15
10
5
0
Films
Blind Date
Beadle
Saint & Greavsie
09:30
12:30
15:30
18:30
21:30
00:30
Business People
ABC1 Men

Figure 7   Sunday

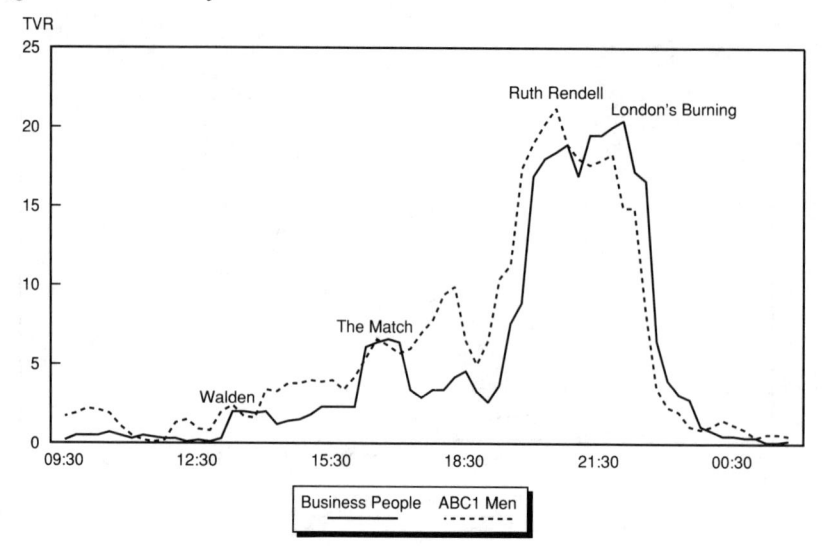

Business People: A Thames Television Survey October 1990
Source: BMRB/Thames/BARB

Appendix 4

These two illustrations represent exactly the kind of advertising that Thames wished to carry and, as a result of BMRB's research, did carry.

Reproduced by kind permission of the LDDC from their television commercial, featured in a campaign planned and booked by Media Campaign Services.

Reproduced by kind permission of Apricot Computers Ltd and their advertising agency Alliance International (London) Ltd.

6

ADAS

PROFESSIONAL SERVICES IN AGRICULTURE

SUMMARY

ADAS has the highest level of spontaneous awareness as a source of advice available to farmers in England.

ADAS, the Agricultural Development and Advisory Service of the Ministry of Agriculture, Fisheries and Food (MAFF), operates throughout England and Wales providing all types of farmers with a range of advisory services.

Since 1987, many of the services provided by ADAS have been charged. Certain types of advice for the 'public good' on conservation, pollution control, diversification and animal welfare are provided free of charge.

ADAS is in the process of restructuring and had identified the need for market research in developing its future commercial strategy.

Separately, the National Audit Office (NAO) was planning an examination of the advisory services of MAFF.

The NAO reports directly to the Public Accounts Committee of the House of Commons and is totally independent of government.

Due to the non-availability of criteria allowing reliable assessment of the profitability on various activities, market research was to be commissioned by the NAO as part of the study. With the coincidence of the need of both organisations for market research they agreed to propose a joint project.

The proposal argued for a two-stage project. The first stage involving group discussions; the second stage would be a quantitative study of 1,000 telephone interviews with farmers.

The full survey was to cover farming practices in England. However, for NAO purposes, a similar exercise was to be carried out in Scotland.

The following discussion covers only the output from the survey of farmers in England.

Nearly a half of all farmers had bought some type of advice. ADAS was the market leader based on numbers of farmers using the service. However, they spent a much lower amount on ADAS advice than they were likely to spend on more specialist services. The ADAS service was generating lower volume incomes on the advice it was giving.

The survey also showed the areas where farmers bought advice from ADAS and all other organisations providing general or specialist services.

The overall perception by farmers towards ADAS was positive.

The survey provided both the NAO and ADAS with strong, actionable information.

The NAO have reported on many of the measures in their report – *Advisory Services to Agriculture*, Report by the Controller and Auditor General.

Both ADAS and the NAO has been very positive about the role of market research.

In the case of the NAO it reconfirmed their belief that market research provides an effective method for evaluating public attitudes to government services.

Whilst having carried out research on previous value-for-money services, this was the first time that the NAO had commissioned research as a fully-integrated, but discrete part of an examination.

The ADAS are actually using the research in the planning of their commercial strategies.

New services are being developed as a result of this project. ADAS clearly sees market research playing a more significant role as part of its future marketing strategy.

*   *   *   *   *

INTRODUCTION

This paper describes a market research project that was jointly funded by the National Audit Office (NAO) and the Agricultural Development and Advisory Service (ADAS). The project was designed to evaluate farmers' attitudes to, and usage of, the full range of advisory services available to them.

BACKGROUND TO THE CLIENTS

National Audit Office

The NAO employs some 900 staff and is headed up by the Comptroller and Auditor General.

He and the NAO are totally independent of government and report directly to the Public Accounts Committee of the House of Commons. He certifies the accounts of all government departments and a wide range of other public sector bodies, and he has statutory authority to report to Parliament on the economy, efficiency and effectiveness with which departments and other bodies use their resources.

Agricultural Development and Advisory Service (ADAS)

It has long been an important role for the Ministry of Agriculture, Fisheries and Food (MAFF) to provide advice to farmers. This advice is provided in England and Wales by ADAS. (In Scotland, advisory services to farmers are provided by the Scottish Agricultural Colleges, an independent organisation which is grant-aided by the Scottish Office Agriculture and Fisheries Department.)

Currently ADAS has an advisory staff of some 1,650 and costs around £53 million per annum (including support staff).

Some of the staff are based at the headquarters in London, but most are located with other MAFF staff in a network of regional and divisional offices throughout England and Wales.

ADAS also provides policy advice to agriculture ministers, and carries out research and development, various other statutory work, and until fiscal 1990-91, included the State Veterinary Service.

In 1989-90 ADAS employed in total (including the State Veterinary Service) around 3,800 staff, together with a further 1,300 Ministry support staff at a cost of around £157 million.

Through ADAS, ministers aim to foster an efficient, market-oriented and environmentally conscious agriculture industry.

BACKGROUND TO THE RESEARCH PROJECT

Prior to 1987 the advisory service of ADAS was provided free of charge. In April 1987 ADAS introduced charges for many types of advice, for some statutory animal health work and for contract research and development. Ministers decided that certain advice for the 'public good' should continue to be free of charge. This 'public good' advice includes initial advice on conservation, the environment and diversification of business. It also covers advice on environmental and socio-economic issues provided in conjunction with chargeable advice.

During 1990-91 a restructuring of ADAS was announced by Ministers. Changes will be carried out by two 'Next Steps' executive agencies during 1992. One agency will cover the field research and advisory activities.

This agency is expected to become a trading fund and achieve full cost recovery on its commercial works. It is also considered by ministers to be a suitable candidate, in the longer term, for privatisation.

Separately, the National Audit Office (NAO) was planning an investigation into MAFF with particular attention to the advisory service provided by ADAS.

The NAO set out to examine:

In England

- whether the Ministry have adequately defined the objectives and strategy for the advisory work of ADAS, and put in place the necessary planning and management information systems.

- how the Ministry have managed their advisory services, with particular regard to the achievement of targets, the development of the market for commercial work, the deployment of resources, and the provision of 'public good' advice.

A significant part of the NAO examination involved its own staff carrying out extensive interviews with ADAS personnel in England as well as reviewing case histories of advice given to English farmers. Opinions were also sought from interested organisations such as the Countryside Commission, the Council for the Protection of Rural England and others. However, there was no reliable way of internally assessing which activities were making, and could make, the greatest contribution to cost recovery. Also there is now a plethora of commercial organisations providing chargeable advice to farmers. There was also the need to determine farmers' attitudes to those organisations offering advice.

The requirements of ADAS were more directed towards the commercial pressures that were being exerted on business development and planning. Since 1987 ADAS had started to make use of marketing techniques to focus efforts on areas of greatest potential. ADAS had identified the need for further market research to assist in the targeting of this activity.

The needs of ADAS and the NAO to undertake market research coincided and they jointly proposed and funded a project to survey farmers' use of advice.

The NAO has used market research in the past. This research had been a major part of a value-for-money study.

This was the first time they had commissioned research as a fully-integrated discrete part of an examination dealing with agricultural expenditure.

THE RESEARCH BRIEF

The objectives set out in the research brief were:

- To assess the impact and value of ADAS advice to the farming industry to inform a report to Parliament on the value obtained for the public expenditure on the advisory service.

- To assess developments in ADAS's marketing effectiveness.

- To provide background information on the market for agricultural advice, and ADAS's position within it, with particular reference to ADAS's potential cost recovery in future.

- To provide information to assist ADAS in its continuing efforts to market services effectively to farmers.

The brief also outlined the type of survey the NAO and ADAS had in mind:

> "A quantitative survey of farmer users and potential users of the service, using telephone interviewing, accompanied questionnaire or a

combination of the two. A sample size of between 500 and 1,000. A draft survey outline is set out below. Contact names and addresses would be provided to the market research company."

For the purposes of the NAO alone, a similar survey was to be carried out in Scotland.

OBJECTIVES OF THE RESEARCH

In considering the brief, we believed that the research could be defined, in broad terms, by two objectives:

- To assess the value and impact of ADAS advice to the farming industry, and to inform and report to Parliament on the value obtained from public expenditure on the service, and
- to provide information to ADAS as to its current standing amongst the target sectors for its services, which would assist in planning future promotional and marketing activity.

The research was designed to provide ADAS and the NAO with:

- an understanding of the levels of awareness and usage that farmers have/make of the various sources of advice available to them.
- an indication of the awareness which exists amongst the target market of the various services provided by ADAS; and what usage levels (by segment) there are for the various services.
- perceptions of the strengths and weaknesses of ADAS and the other sources of advice available, which should help both in the future tailoring of services and in the way they are promoted.
- an understanding of what likely future trends there would be for advice on the farm.
- a profile of farmers who purchase advice from ADAS, together with a profile of those who seek advice from elsewhere. This should help to identify areas where ADAS may consider improving or extending its services.

Essentially we were proposing a study which provided both in-depth and quantitative measures.

THE RESEARCH APPROACH

Our strong recommendation was, therefore, that the research objectives would best be met by a combination of traditional qualitative research and quantitative telephone interviews in a two-stage approach.

Initially, group discussions with farmers would be the vehicle for carrying out the qualitative stage of the survey. Telephone interviews would form the second, quantitative, phase of the survey.

The group discussions would provide a real understanding of the underlying attitudes and motivations which prevail in respect of ADAS and other advisory services. They would also yield several other benefits, particularly in the assistance they would provide in the development of the questionnaire for the quantitative phase. This was especially the case when usage dimensions/constructs would be required.

Telephone interviewing with farmers is a widely accepted form of interviewing. Many farmers have taken part in research surveys in the past. For agricultural surveys, telephone interviewing is normally preferred because farm locations tend to be very widely distributed and because telephone interviewing permits a wider distribution of respondents than is normally possible in personal, face-to-face interviewing where clustering of the sample tends to take place. The interviews were to be carried out using computer-assisted telephone interviewing (CATI).

It will be noted that this *approach* reflected a significant change to the brief. It may be recalled that the NAO and ADAS envisaged a quantitative survey only. However, BJM's arguments were well received by the clients and they were satisfied as to the benefits of adopting the research approach proposed.

The discussion on the design of the project and the sample structure for both the qualitative and quantitative stages will be found in the Appendix.

OUTPUT FROM THE RESEARCH

General

There is a large volume of commercially sensitive information contained in these reports which ADAS, in particular, wished to remain confidential.

However, there are certain elements of information which the NAO have included in their report to Parliament* which is now in the public domain.

The NAO and the Board of ADAS received full detailed presentations on both stages of the report. As far as the quantitative section was concerned, ADAS received only the data for England.

SUMMARY OF RESEARCH FINDINGS

We are not in a position to review the output from the qualitative phase other than to comment that some of the issues raised were incorporated into the questionnaire for the quantitative stage.

The main discussion is based on the 750 interviews carried out with English farmers.

The Market for Charged Advice

It has been mentioned earlier that one of the key requirements for both ADAS and the NAO from this study was to define the size of the market for advice, information not previously available.

The questionnaire was structured to allow the spend on the many and varied organisations providing charged advice to be estimated. The findings showed that:

- 44% of farmers had paid for advice in the previous 12 months.

- 43% of those buying advice had purchased it from ADAS. This gave it market leader status based on this measure. Accountants (31%), vets (22%) and solicitors (14%) were the other suppliers most widely used for paid-for advice.

- Charged advice for farm management, and animal production was the most widely sought.

- The average annual spend on ADAS advice was estimated at £368 compared to an average spend over all suppliers of £1,235. Thus, ADAS advice accounted for 30% of the value of all advice given.

It can therefore be seen that, whilst overall ADAS had a strong representation with farmers, the services it was providing were generating lower volume incomes.

**Advisory Services to Agriculture*, Report by the Comptroller and Auditor General HC.358 £6.70 HMSO.

The survey also showed the areas in which farmers paid for advice from ADAS and other organisations.

Just over 30% of all purchased advice in the previous 12 months was on farm management-type requirements. ADAS had around a fifth by value of that market.

Next, in decreasing order, were animal production, arable, buildings and machinery, and the least of the top five areas for spend was horticulture. Overall, these five categories accounted for 72% of all advice purchased. Horticulture represented around 3% by value, but ADAS had around three-quarters of this market. ADAS appeared to be stronger in the smaller markets and weaker in the larger markets.

It is important to consider one further point at this stage. It has always been considered in agriculture that the arable sector has a significant demand for advice, especially for fertilizer, herbicide, fungicide and insecticide usage. Theoretically this demand should make it one of the strongest markets and it is one to which ADAS has targeted its resources. The reality is that the suppliers of these products – the merchants and chemical specialists – provide advice as part of their service to arable farmers. This advice is perceived by farmers to be free. Although they acknowledge that it is accounted for in the price of the chemicals they purchase, it is still perceived to be *free*.

Consequently, arable farmers are likely to utilise this 'free' service on those particular issues rather than pay for advice from ADAS. There are other areas where farmers are likely to pay for advice and these were identified in the qualitative phase, e.g. succession planning, taxation.

Effectiveness of ADAS

69% of all farmers were able to mention ADAS spontaneously as a source of advice, representing the highest level of awareness for organisations providing advice.

Overall, the charged-for advice supplied by ADAS was rated as relevant, and provided value for money. Predictably, the more specialist sources (e.g. vets and surveyors) achieved scores above average. The score for ADAS for both measures was slightly below the average, but, given the greater number of farmers using their services, this was considered to be a satisfactory performance.

In all cases of charged advice there was a high level of potential repeat business. In the case of ADAS, nine out of ten farmers who had used their service are likely to use their service in the future. This level of repeat buying provides an element of confidence in the relationship of ADAS with the farmer.

The survey was also able to show that as far as non-customers of ADAS were concerned, there had been an apparently low level of activity to recruit new users.

Of those farmers who had not used ADAS, only around one-fifth had any contact with ADAS and, in the case of 80% of them, *they* had made the contact. This meant that ADAS was only getting directly to less than 5% of non-users. Those that had made contact found it easy and convenient.

In the overall prediction for the future development of charged advice, farmers indicated that their buying intentions were likely to be in the areas of animal health and welfare, arable and horticultural crop production and business management. Around two-thirds of all farmers, and three-quarters of existing customers, would consider using ADAS for this advice. In the area of pollution advice, 90% of farmers are likely to turn to ADAS.

'Public Good' Advice

The main areas of 'public good' advice in agriculture are pollution control, nature conservation, animal welfare and diversification.

Just over a third of all farmers had sought advice on 'public good' matters at some time. Pollution control, at 16% of all farmers, was the most frequently requested; diversification at 11% was the least frequently requested. Overall, ADAS provided around a third of this advice.

Other organisations that farmers turned to for 'public good' advice included: Farming and Wildlife Advisory Group (FWAG); National Rivers Authority and local Water Boards; Nature Conservancy Council (NCC); the farmer's vet and the local council.

84% of all farmers receiving 'public good' advice had followed, or were in the process of following, the advice received.

Just under 60% of users of this advice had received it in connection with grant applications.

Around a half of all farmers not in receipt of ADAS 'public good' advice were unaware that they provided that type of advice.

THE EFFECT OF THE RESEARCH

ADAS

The output from the research has been widely used within the organisation in the planning and development of new services. It is expected that ADAS will be refocusing its attention on more profitable business areas, previously not considered, and re-designing other services it offers in its current market segments. New services and product repositionings have already been affected or are being developed as a result of this project.

There is also further commitment to use research more strongly as a marketing tool. Clearly ADAS, as a result of this project, sees research playing a more significant role in its commercial development, in the changing environment in which it is expected to perform.

NAO

The NAO has gained great benefit from the survey as it was able to quantify areas for its own report on ADAS and MAFF, where that data would not otherwise have been available. The output from the research is referred to several times during the report.

Its experience with this survey confirmed its belief that market research, intelligently used, is an effective method for evaluating public attitudes to government services.

APPENDICES

Acknowledgements

The co-operation of the NAO and ADAS is acknowledged, and their approval for this project to be submitted to the AMSO Award scheme, and the inclusion of parts of the NAO report in this document, is greatly appreciated.

Project Design

The project design was required to produce a sample which would reflect the attitudes and behaviour of all registered farmers in mainland England, and in Scotland for the NAO only.

The brief called for the following farm types to be covered: less favoured area (LFA) beef and sheep; lowground beef and sheep; dairy; specialist arable; horticulture.

(Specialist arable essentially covers cereals [wheat and barley], sugar beet, potatoes and oilseed rape. Horticulture covers vegetables, fruits, nursery stock and glasshouse crops.)

Pig and poultry livestock categories were not to be considered in the sample design. One further category to be allowed for in the design of the study was farm size. The MAFF designation of Standard Man Days (SMD) was to be used as a size categorisation, as discussed further below.

Sample Structure

In all, eight group discussions were to be held throughout England and Scotland to cover all the defined categories of farm and to reflect regional variations.

The qualitative stage was to be followed by 1,000 telephone interviews with farmers using a fully-structured questionnaire with a quota sample covering the categories of farm as defined in the brief. As it had not been possible to comment in the qualitative stage, sample details are confined to the quantitative stage.

Structure of Quantitative Phase

As has been stated already, 1,000 telephone interviews were carried out.
The sample had to allow for:

- Regional analysis, including a separate analysis for Scotland.

- classification of farm activity.

- classification by farm size using the category of Standard Man Days (SMD).

A wide range of statistics covering farm size and structure are available. These data are constructed on an annual census of all registered farms in the country, including part-time holdings. Each June, farmers complete a questionnaire on the livestock and crops they are producing.

The data are covered by the Agricultural Statistics Act 1979. Chapter 13, Section 3 of that Act defines the "Restriction on disclosure of information". This section deals with the confidentiality of the data, but allows for certain cases where closer interrogation of the data can be sanctioned.

The published statistics do not provide size category by SMDs – it is by herd size or crop area. Full consultation on the sample structure was maintained with ADAS and the NAO – in particular the statistics branch of the NAO.

It was also a requirement that BJM sign a secrecy agreement before census data were provided.

The procedure outlined above resulted in separate samples being drawn for England and Scotland. It was agreed that 750 interviews would be carried out in England and 250 in Scotland, which meant that Scotland would be over sampled relative to England. A minimum sample of 250 in Scotland was considered adequate for the analysis required.

The actual sample structure in England was defined as:

Table 1

England:		Standard Man Days	
	<250	250-1000	>1000
Dairy }		60	70
Livestock }		60	70
Arable }	100	60	70
Horticulture }		60	70
Other }		60	70
	100	**300**	**350**

All told, 5,000 farmer respondents were provided, i.e. 5 times the actual sample required. This factor of 5 applied to each individual sample segment identified. Each respondent was identified only by their unique farm (holding), parish and county reference number. Names and addresses were provided, but BJM had to source the telephone numbers.

No other information on the characteristics of the respondents' farm was provided. Consequently, the questionnaire had to be structured to collect information to allow respondents to be included in the correct category for both farm type and size.

This was not as straightforward as may at first sight seem to be the case. In the overall classification of farm type, several categories are defined, into which a holding is allocated, depending on enterprise specialisation, e.g. dairying, cropping, general livestock etc. As an example, there are two categories for dairy: 'specialist dairy' and 'mainly dairy'. 'Specialist dairy' is when more than 70% of the SMDs are allocated to the dairy herd. 'Mainly dairy' is where between 50% and 70% of SMDs are allocated to dairying. In the defined sample these two categories are combined under the heading 'dairy'.

The other categories that were defined, and would be subject to separate analysis, were: arable, general livestock (beef and sheep) and horticulture.

The SMD for each holding is calculated by using a model that was established in 1976. Standard labour requirements are assessed against all types of crop and livestock production. For example, it is assumed that each hectare of wheat produced requires 2.5 SMDs; each cow and heifer in milk in the dairy herd requires 7.0 SMDs. In the treatment of the data, it is widely accepted that 250 SMDs equal one permanent, full time worker.

As BJM were not able to be exposed to the full information on each respondent, a procedure had to be developed for allocating each into a size and farm-type cell. The procedure that was adopted was for BJM to calculate the category to which each respondent should be allocated by collecting appropriate data in the interim, and then applying a model based on the standard labour requirement criteria referred to earlier.

Certain crop areas and livestock numbers were to be collected as the first stage of the questionnaire and the SMD calculated for them. The computer then allocated the respondent into the respective cell.

There was an inherent risk in this approach as it was unlikely that this procedure would fully simulate the official model. The 20 minute interview allowed only limited crop and livestock details to be evaluated compared with the extremely wide range of variables measured in the census.

To allow an accurate assessment to be made, it was agreed that at the end of the telephoning stage the unique reference number for each respondent would be allocated into the 'correct' category. BJM would not be exposed to this analysis.

A matrix was returned showing the achieved sample structure.

The predicted sample structure, using the model developed by BJM in the questionnaire, is shown below for the English part of the survey.

Table 2

England		Standard Man Days		
		<250	250-1000	>1000
Dairy	}		120	52
Livestock	}		81	22
Arable	}	156	93	37
Horticulture	}		34	43
Others	}		39	76
		156	**367**	**230**

This predicted sample structure appears to indicate that both the smaller farm sizes, and dairy and arable farms as defined by SMD, were over-sampled in the BJM survey.

However, the returned analysis of the *actual* characteristics of the sample achieved the following sample structure:

Table 3

England:		Standard Man Days	
	<250	250-1000	>1000
Dairy }		77	90
Livestock }		82	92
Arable }	58	66	59
Horticulture }		50	47
Others }		66	60
	58	341	348

Note: Because of the way the data were handled, totals in the above tables will not match the earlier ones. The projection is based on statistical treatment of the first 150 references randomly selected.

This indicates that smaller farms were slightly under sampled in England, but that in other respects the achieved sample was reasonably close to the original requirement.

In comparing the sample structure predicted by the BJM model with that which was actually achieved, the collective view of all parties was that the BJM prediction was statistically acceptable. The conclusion was reached that any further resource allocation would provide only a marginal improvement in the statistical interpretation of the data.

Table 4

England:		Standard Man Days	
	<250	250-1000	>1000
Dairy }		16,215	7,996
Livestock }		13,483	1,951
Arable }	89,139*	12,300	5,187
Horticulture }		5,810	4,570
Other }		–	–
Total 156,651 (157,393)			

Note: *includes 'others' equal to 4,279

During the whole process, respondent confidentiality was fully retained.

Weighting factors were applied to each category based on the actual sample universe. The universe is based on the number of farms.

The fully weighted sample structure shown in Table 4 was obtained. The figures in parenthesis represent the true universe.

Both ADAS and NAO received copies of both weighted and unweighted tabulation. ADAS only received data for England.

7

HOME OFFICE

FROM DOLL'S HOUSE TO DYING – ALARMINGLY EFFECTIVE RESEARCH

SUMMARY

The Home Office's Publicity Campaign for fire safety has for the past 3 years concentrated on convincing the general public that smoke fumes are the main danger in house fires and that installing a smoke alarm should be a priority. The objective is to have 70% of homes in England and Wales owning an installed smoke alarm by 1994.

After several years of advertising featuring the dangers of chip pans, cigarettes etc., the smoke alarm campaign opened with a TV advert known as *Doll's House,* which was tested in one television region at the beginning of 1988 and shown in two TV regions during December 1988 and January 1989. A research monitor was commissioned from BJM Research & Consultancy Ltd by Central Office of Information to gauge changes in attitudes to smoke alarms, and to see if these could be attributed to the effect of the campaign. The first of these monitors was in Spring 1989.

Because of its success *Doll's House* was shown again in all TV regions in the Winter of 1989/1990. The second monitor was carried out in February/March 1990 and showed again a broadly successful and effective campaign particularly amongst families with children and the middle classes.

However, it also clearly demonstrated that there was a group which was particularly difficult to reach, who appeared not to be influenced to the same extent by the *Doll's House* campaign. These were the older people (aged over 55 years) and especially the downmarket older people.

The effect of this research taken together with an analysis of fire statistics was to persuade the Home Office to change its overt target audience to the older age group whose attitudes and likelihood of installing a smoke alarm were not improving at the same speed as the other age groups.

As a result of this, a new advert call *Dying* was made to target the older and lower socio-economic sectors of the public. This was shown in all TV regions in England and Wales during the Winter of 1990/91. It aimed particularly at motivating the groups who were showing greater resistance – the elderly; those in private rented homes; and the lower socio-economic groups.

There had been some pressure on the Home Office to review *Doll's House* which, because of complaints to the television authority, could only be shown at certain times. This could have made it difficult for the Home Office to achieve the number of TVRs that it had targeted.

This paper demonstrates the role that research played in that review, which changed the target for the advertising from families with children to the elderly and lower socio-economic groups.

Without this evidence, having only otherwise penetration data, the Home Office would have been reluctant to change from a seemingly very effective communication approach. The research carried out established the need to address the older group directly and on their own terms.

The research method employed was relatively straightforward, consisting of a survey of heads of household or spouse carried out in the Spring of 1989, which was repeated and expanded in the Springs of 1990 and 1991. Sample sizes of 1,475, 2,093 and 2,128 adults were interviewed in each year respectively. Interviewing was carried out in the home, using structured questionnaires.

Doll's House was shown throughout England and Wales at the beginning of 1990, although complications were introduced by the screening of other fire prevention advertising by local Fire and Civil Defence Associations.

The research carried out in February 1990 following the first national (England and Wales) showing of *Doll's House* demonstrated that the advertising was very effective in reaching families with children. This group was likely to be the easiest one to persuade to buy and install smoke alarms and so get the smoke alarm ball rolling. The groups which showed the most resistance to buying and installing smoke alarms were the elderly and downmarket groups. Amongst these groups, in addition, there was a high level of reliance on pets, particularly dogs, to wake their owners in case of fire during the night.

Based on these research findings the focus of the advertising was switched for the 1991 campaign to address the problem of persuading the elderly to buy and install smoke alarms.

Further research has shown that, because of the changes in the campaign, the attitudes of elderly people to house fires and their likelihood to buy smoke alarms have improved.

The research has thus been effective in changing the advertising, which in turn has encouraged more people of all age groups to install smoke alarms, and thus saved more lives than might otherwise have been the case.

* * * * *

BUSINESS BACKGROUND

Fire prevention publicity at a national level in England and Wales is the responsibility of the Home Office which, over the years, has adopted a number of different strategies to create awareness of the dangers of fire in the home and to help thereby save lives and property. Such campaigns have, in the past, featured the dangers of chip pans or cigarettes, for example, and their associated fire risk, or the importance of getting quickly out of a house on fire because of the speed with which a fire can spread.

Fire Brigades have a responsibility for fire prevention publicity at a local level.

During the latter part of the 1980s cheaper domestic smoke alarms came onto the market and became widely available. In 1987 the Home Office decided to promote the installation of smoke alarms in private households on the basis that a smoke alarm can alert the occupants to a house fire before it becomes too late to get out safely, and so reduce loss of life.

The initial strategy was to target the communication at families with children.

This route was chosen because qualitative research had suggested that whilst both older people and children were groups at risk, featuring children at risk in the advertising would have a broader and more emotive appeal. At that point in time, ownership of smoke alarms was very low and it was important that advertising should have the broadest possible appeal in order to stimulate an almost non-existent market.

An advertisement, *Doll's House*, was developed by the advertising agency FCO and shown in the North East television region at the beginning of 1988. In the rest of England and Wales, the previous strategy using the campaign *Bucket* was continued. Evaluation of *Doll's House* by pre- and post-advertising research showed that it was achieving the desired communication objectives. Consequently, its use was changed to the London and Lancashire TV areas for the beginning of 1989, and to the whole of England and Wales for 1990.

THE ROLE OF RESEARCH

It was always recognised by the Home Office and the COI that research would play a significant role in both formulating the campaign and shaping its progress.

Qualitative research was carried out in order to develop the campaign and the *Doll's House* treatment was shown in a single television region with pre- and post-research carried out to test its effectiveness there.

The sponsor of the advertising, the Home Office, is obviously not a manufacturer or retailer of smoke alarms, the products that the campaign was designed to promote, so sales figures were not going to be easy to compile.

Penetration data to measure how many homes had installed a smoke alarm was commissioned from AGB Home Audits.

But penetration figures alone would be insufficient to explain any differentials between various groups. Nor would they explain how or why attitudes were or were not changing amongst groups in which the penetration failed to improve at a satisfactory rate.

Research, then, would be required to monitor these changes, and changes in attitudes towards house fires and smoke alarms, to ensure that the campaign maintained maximum effectiveness.

BJM Research & Consultancy Ltd was subsequently commissioned by the Central Office of Information to carry out an appropriate research study.

Post campaign research was carried out in the Spring of 1989 to monitor the effectiveness of the advertising in terms of creating awareness of fire precautions and knowledge about fires, and to measure attitudes to smoke alarms and intention to purchase.

The findings of that research were generally favourable. The penetration of smoke alarms in private households began to increase, and was shown to be higher in the two areas which had received the advertising than it was in the country as a whole.

The campaign was extended to cover the whole of England and Wales at the beginning of 1990 and the monitor was repeated in the Spring of 1990.

It is with the Spring 1990 survey and its effect on the development of the campaign that this paper is primarily concerned.

ISSUES AND OBJECTIVES

The aim of the Home Office is to increase the penetration of smoke alarms in domestic property to as high a level as possible in order to save lives that might otherwise be lost in house fires. From a base of 10% penetration in 1987, the Home Office has set a target of achieving 70% penetration by 1994.

It was recognised early in the life of the campaign that there would be likely to be certain people with a relatively high resistance to installing a smoke alarm. Identification of this group, and specifically targeting publicity at them, would be likely to be necessary at some point in the campaign if the penetration target was to be met.

Research was therefore required following the 1990 campaign to monitor the effect of the campaign in terms of changing attitudes amongst both the adult population as a whole and amongst specific target groups in order to determine which, if any, groups responded more positively to the campaign, and which showed no, or relatively little, movement in their attitudes.

The objectives which were therefore set for the 1990 research were:

- to monitor awareness of fire prevention precautions and knowledge about fires.

- to measure attitudes to smoke alarms.

- to measure intention to purchase smoke alarms amongst non-owners.

- to check awareness of, and reactions to, the advertising.

RESEARCH METHOD

A straightforward research approach was adopted.

The relevant universe was defined as being heads of household or spouses on the basis that either of these could purchase, or influence a purchase of, smoke alarms for the home.

In the survey carried out in February 1989, when *Doll's House* had been shown only in London and Lancashire television regions, sample sizes of

200 had been adopted in each of these regions. These two regions had needed to be evaluated separately because, in advance of Home Office sponsored advertising, *Doll's House* had already been shown in London in Spring and Autumn of 1988, paid for by the London Fire and Civil Defence Association. No benchmark study had been carried out in London prior to these screenings of *Doll's House*.

For control purposes, and to provide benchmark data for the rest of the country, a 200 interview sample size had also been adopted for each of the Yorkshire and Midland television regions, and 100 in each of East of England, Southern, South West, and Wales and the West television regions. Because of its history as the pilot test region for *Doll's House* in 1988, a sample of 200 had been decided on for the North East, although the advertisement had not been on air in that region in 1989.

At the analysis stage, weighting had been applied to the data to restore each television region to its correct proportion by size of adult population in order to give a total England and Wales picture.

Within each television region interviewing was carried out in randomly selected wards with quota controls set by sex interlocked with age, social class, tenure and type of dwelling.

For the 1990 survey the same approach was adopted with the exception that sample sizes of 200 were adopted for each of the ten television regions covering England and Wales (including the relevant part of the Border region).

Interviewing was carried out in-home and interviews lasted approximately 30 minutes.

THE SUCCESS

The proportion of homes with an installed smoke alarm was shown by the AGB Home Audit data to have increased significantly between early 1989 and early 1990, from 23% in March 1989 to 31% in March 1990.

The BJM monitor also showed that awareness of the risks of fire had increased; that awareness of the role of smoke alarms had increased; and that, of the people without a smoke alarm, more than the previous year said that they would be likely to install one.

First, and most important, the pool of people with no positive intention to buy a smoke alarm had decreased. In 1989 37% did not own a smoke alarm, and had either not heard of them or had no positive intention to buy one. In 1990 that had fallen to 29%.

Knowledge of where to install smoke alarms had also increased. Recommended points of installation for smoke alarms are on the ceiling in a hallway, at the bottom of the stairs, or at the top of the stairs. Amongst people who had heard of smoke alarms, whether they had one installed or not, the proportion who mentioned the ceiling as the appropriate place increased from 74% to 81%, and the proportion mentioning the hallway increased from 51% to 58%. Both of these increases were greater than could be accounted for simply by the increased penetration.

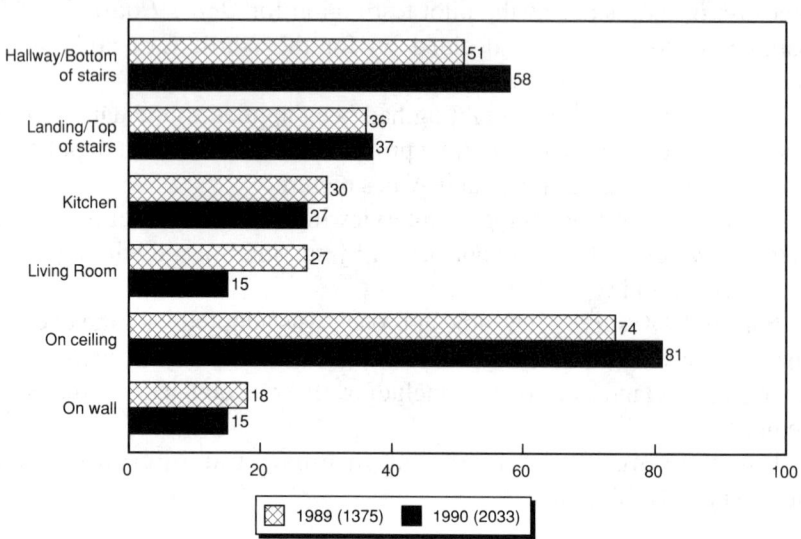

Figure 1   Where in your home would you fit a smoke alarm?

	1989 (1375)	1990 (2033)
Hallway/Bottom of stairs	51	58
Landing/Top of stairs	36	37
Kitchen	30	27
Living Room	27	15
On ceiling	74	81
On wall	18	15

Base: All aware of smoke alarms (%)

Appreciation of the speed with which smoke can fill a house had also improved. The average expected time fell from 6.3 minutes to 5.9 minutes. This was particularly pleasing given that the *Doll's House* advertisement deliberately tried to convey the idea that smoke can spread rapidly. (See Figure 2).

Coupled with this was a decrease in the length of time which it was thought would be taken for someone to die from smoke inhalation. The average expected time fell from 6.6 minutes to 5.6 minutes.

Clearly the campaign was being successful, but the 1990 survey also identified a worrying aspect of that success.

Figure 2
Length of time taken for smoke and fumes to fill home

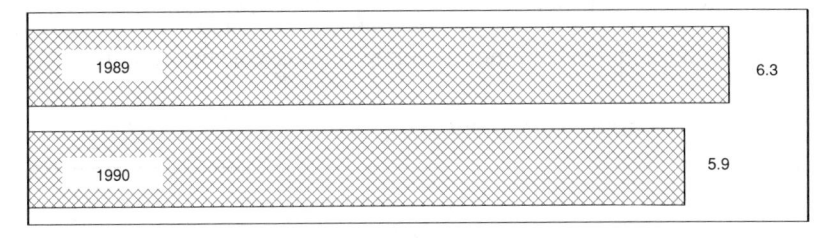

Year	Minutes
1989	6.3
1990	5.9

Length of time taken for someone to die from smoke inhalation

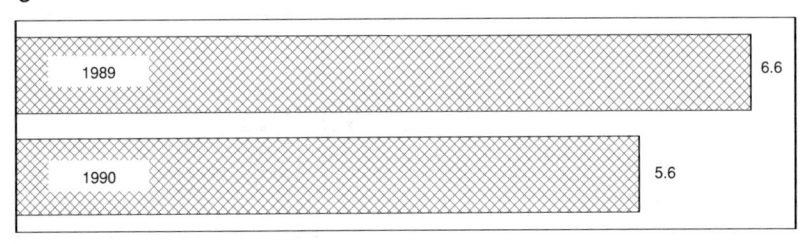

Year	Minutes
1989	6.6
1990	5.6

Base: All respondents 1989 (1,475), 1990 (2,093)
Note: Mean time given (minutes)

THE PROBLEM

The penetration of smoke alarms in private homes was shown by the AGB data to be rising more slowly in the homes of older people than in those of younger people. On this evidence it might have been supposed that the older target group would increase their penetration of smoke alarms but more slowly.

However, the BJM survey showed that this was unlikely to happen if only *Doll's House* was used.

By being able to look beyond behaviour (i.e. installation) to examine attitudes amongst the different age groups it became apparent that older people:

- appeared to misunderstand the message of *Doll's House*, and their perception that they were at risk actually went down.
- failed to appreciate the speed with which smoke can spread and can kill.

- would be less willing to leave the home in the event of a fire.
- had a misplaced confidence in their own or their pet's ability to detect smoke in good time.
- showed no increase in inclination to purchase a smoke alarm.

Figure 3   Ownership and Intent

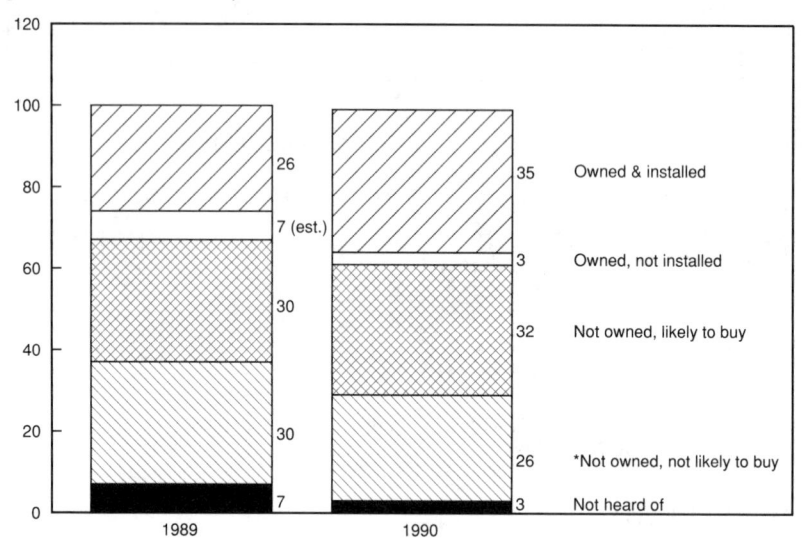

Category	1989	1990
Owned & installed	26	35
Owned, not installed	7 (est.)	3
Not owned, likely to buy	30	32
*Not owned, not likely to buy	30	26
Not heard of	7	3

Note: * Includes might not buy and don't know

The Spread of Smoke

As reported in the previous section, one of the apparent successes of the campaign was to reduce the expected time that it would take for smoke to fill a house. However, when this was examined by age group it was found that the movement was largely amongst younger people. Older people (over 55 years old was taken as the definition of the older age group in order to give a robust base of over 700 respondents) not only expected smoke to fill a home more slowly than did younger people, thus expecting to have more time to evacuate a building on fire, but their expectation had not moved significantly between the 1989 and 1990 surveys.

In 1989 the average time expected by the over-55 year-old age group for smoke to fill a home was 7.4 minutes, 1.8 minutes longer than the 16 to 34 year-old age group (5.6 minutes). In 1990 the 16 to 34 year-olds had shortened their average expected time to 4.4 minutes, but that of the over-55 year-olds remained virtually unchanged at 7.2 minutes. The difference in expectation between the two age groups had extended to 2.8 minutes.

Figure 4 Length of time taken for smoke and fumes to fill home

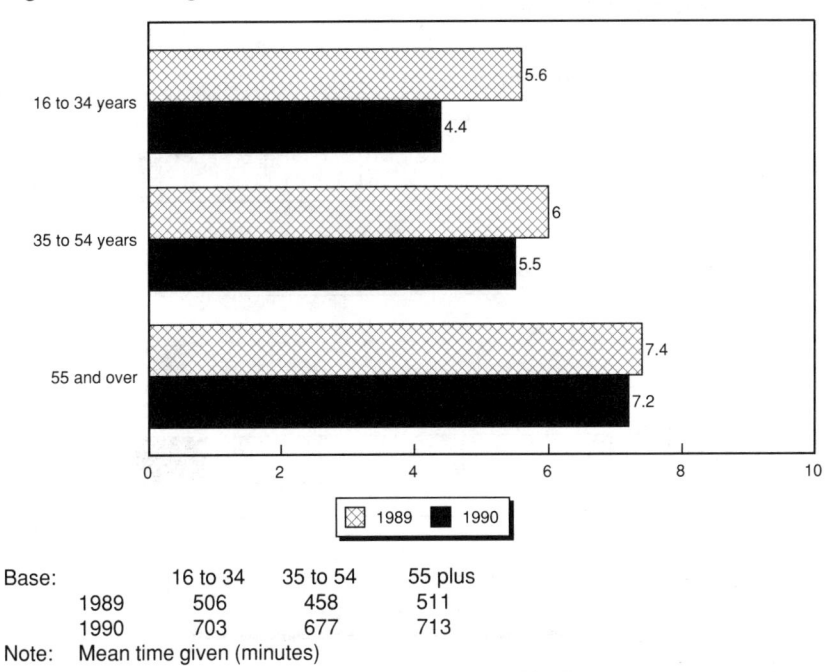

Age group	1989	1990
16 to 34 years	5.6	4.4
35 to 54 years	6	5.5
55 and over	7.4	7.2

Base:

	16 to 34	35 to 54	55 plus
1989	506	458	511
1990	703	677	713

Note: Mean time given (minutes)

It appeared that the younger age group was absorbing the message that smoke fills a house faster than you expect, but this was not being taken on board by the older age group.

Complacency

A greater complacency amongst the older group was also suggested by a number of other pieces of data.

They were less likely to say that they would leave their home if it was on fire than the younger age groups and more likely to say they would tackle it or try and save possessions. Penetration of installed smoke alarms was lowest amongst this age group (six percentage points below the average) and, as alarmingly, future intention to purchase was lowest here and not showing any improvement year on year.

Intention to Purchase an Alarm

This was the only age group in which more people without a smoke alarm said that they would not be likely to buy a smoke alarm in the future than said that they would be likely to buy one. 40% of the over-55 year-olds without an alarm said that they would definitely or probably not buy a smoke alarm, compared to 36% who would.

Figure 5   Intention to purchase a smoke alarm 1990

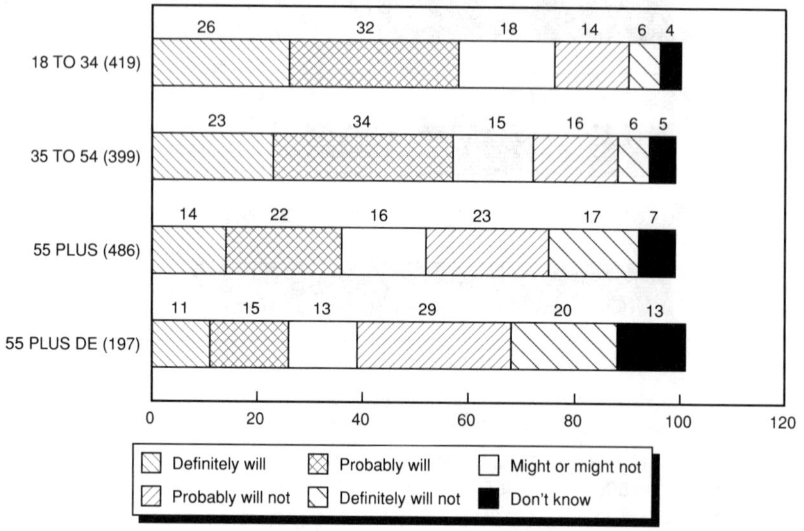

Age group	Definitely will	Probably will	Might or might not	Probably will not	Definitely will not	Don't know
18 TO 34 (419)	26	32	18	14	6	4
35 TO 54 (399)	23	34	15	16	6	5
55 PLUS (486)	14	22	16	23	17	7
55 PLUS DE (197)	11	15	13	29	20	13

Base: All not currently owning a smoke alarm

Amongst a sub-group of this, the over-55 year-olds in social classes DE, the figures were even worse, at 49% and 26% respectively.

There was clearly a problem amongst this group.

It might have been a problem of the perceived cost of smoke alarms that stopped this group from buying, but as the actual cost of alarms fell over this period, so did the perceived cost amongst all age groups. At an average of £12.42, the cost perception amongst the over-55 year-olds was not significantly more than that of the other age groups.

There might have been a problem of tenure, because they had the lowest rate of owner occupancy, and it was clear that people in rented accommodation would be more difficult to persuade to take the responsibility to install alarms than would owner occupiers. But with 58% of this age group owning their own property, this was not significantly less than the 60% of 16 to 34 year-olds and certainly could not account for much the larger difference in both behaviour and intentions.

It appeared that there was a problem of motivation amongst this age group. Whilst attitudes and knowledge were improving significantly amongst the younger age groups, there was little or no movement amongst older people.

If the movement in the younger age groups was attributable to *Doll's House*, it was not having the same effect on older people.

Advertising Communication

Respondents who remembered seeing the *Doll's House* advertisement after prompting with a story board were asked what they thought the main message of it was intended to be. Only 39% of the over-55 year-olds said that they thought the message was that they should buy a smoke alarm compared to 55% of the 16 to 34 year-olds. And when asked to say which of a number of phrases applied to the advertisement only 23% of the over-55 year-olds chose "It has made me think about buying a smoke alarm" compared to 32% of 16 to 34 year-olds.

This provided further evidence that the advertisement was not reaching the older age groups to the same extent that it was getting its message over to younger people.

Groups at Risk

A further cause for concern was that the focus of the advertisement on children being at risk might make others forget that older people are also at risk. This concern was raised by the fact that, when asked which age groups were most at risk in a fire in the home, 91% of respondents had said "the elderly" in 1989, but this fell to 76% in 1990. The proportion saying "children and babies" had, however, remained virtually static at 80% and 79% respectively.

In addition to not communicating to older people, the advertisement could be accused of actually acting against the interest of the elderly by taking attention away from them.

THE 'WAKING' PROBLEM

In the 1990 survey respondents were asked what or who they would expect to wake them in case there was a fire in their home during the night. Owners of smoke alarms mostly said that the first thing that would wake them would be their smoke alarm. Amongst non-owners of alarms the most frequently given first answer was "the smell of the smoke" (58%).

Figure 6   If there were a fire in your home while you were asleep, what do you think would waken you? (1990)

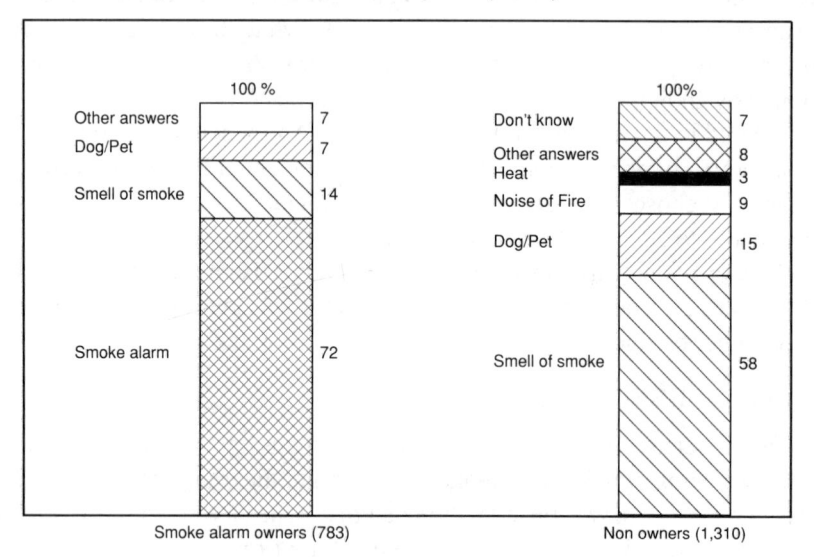

Smoke alarm owners (783)	%	Non owners (1,310)	%
Other answers	7	Don't know	7
Dog/Pet	7	Other answers	8
Smell of smoke	14	Heat	3
		Noise of Fire	9
		Dog/Pet	15
Smoke alarm	72	Smell of smoke	58

This seemed to be a rather optimistic answer based on the assumption that they would not be suffocated by the smoke before they awoke, which is actually the more likely outcome.

The second most frequently mentioned method of non-owners being woken was by the dog or other pet. This again was based on the assumption that the dog would wake before being suffocated. These answers were given despite the fact that 97% of non alarm owners had already spontaneously said that the most likely cause of death if someone were trapped in a house in which there was fire would be the smoke, or inhaling the smoke or fumes.

From this evidence it seemed that, despite the lip service paid to the acknowledged main danger, there was still a considerable failure to understand precisely what that danger entailed.

RESEARCH CONCLUSION

The report on the 1990 study concluded that: "Since the awareness of smoke alarms has almost reached the maximum (at 97%), the role of advertising is not to increase awareness, but to trigger purchase in a largely receptive audience.

The effectiveness of the (*Doll's House*) advertisement continues to be limited amongst a small but high risk group – elderly downmarket people, who do not recognise the danger of fire and smoke as fully as other groups and who do not see the need for smoke alarms."

USE OF RESEARCH RESULTS

The research results were a major factor in the decision to implement a change in the target audience for the Home Office campaign in support of smoke alarms.

A new advertisement was produced to be shown in early 1991. This advertisement very specifically addressed the problems identified by the 1990 survey.

The brief for the new advertisement was clearly based on the research findings that older people were failing to receive the message about the dangers of smoke; that they were the most difficult group to encourage to buy a smoke alarm; and that there was a significant level of complacency probably born out of a failure to fully appreciate that smoke can suffocate and kill both people and animals in their sleep without them waking up.

The result was a direct and forceful advertisement from FCO showing an elderly woman and man and a dog being suffocated by smoke whilst asleep.

Versions of the advertisement were produced lasting 30 seconds and 10 seconds and were shown in all television regions in England and Wales from late December 1990 until February 1991.

EFFECT OF THE CHANGED COMMUNICATION APPROACH

The effect of the change in the communication that had been brought about by the 1990 research could only be measured by once again using research.

A further study was therefore carried out in February 1991 following the end of the burst of advertising which started at the end of December 1990. The structure of the survey was similar to that of the 1990 survey. The main

116 Research Works

difference was that the sampling technique was changed from quota sampling to random location sampling in order to give a more rigorous sampling procedure.

Figure 7 Intention to purchase a smoke alarm 1991

	Definitely will	Probably will	Might or might not	Probably will not	Definitely will not	Don't know
18 TO 34 (359)	30	32	17	11	6	4
35 TO 54 (322)	25	42	17	8	3	5
55 PLUS (450)	19	22	14	20	14	11
55 PLUS DE (188)	19	21	12	24	11	13

Base: All not currently owning a smoke alarm

The AGB Home Audit data for March 1991 is not available at the time of writing, but other indications suggest that penetration of smoke alarms installed in private homes has again increased significantly.

However, the real success has come in the change of attitudes and awareness amongst not only the target group, the over-55's, but the continuing changes seen at the younger end of the age spectrum.

The new advertisement now appears to be addressing all age groups.

Of people who recognise a telepictorial storyboard, 60% of the over-55 year-olds spontaneously said that the main message was to get people to buy a smoke alarm. This is not significantly different from the response of the under-55's (64%), whereas there had been a significant difference between the level of under- and over-55 year-olds who had taken this message out of *Doll's House* (39% and 53% respectively).

For the first time more over-55 year-olds without a smoke alarm said that they are likely to buy one than said they are not likely to. The change in the communication targeting appeared to be having the desired effects *both* of changing the attitudes of older people and of continuing to change those of the younger age groups.

The fall in the proportion of adults who see the elderly as being at risk which occurred between 1989 and 1990 (when it dropped from 91% to 76%) had been largely reversed with an increase to 84%.

Finally, the proportion of people who do not have a smoke alarm and who would expect to be woken by the smell of smoke if there was a fire had fallen from 42% to 33%.

All the indications are that the communication needs identified by the research in 1990 are now being successfully met.

CONCLUSION

The *Doll's House* campaign shown on television in 1989 and 1990 was successful in alerting people to the existence of smoke alarms and the role that they could play in their home as a safety measure.

However, the 1990 research showed that the communication was failing to reach and to change the attitudes of older people, a group that is particularly vulnerable to house fires.

Largely as a result of that research, the targeting and message was altered to address this problem. The advertisement that was subsequently shown appears now to be succeeding in reaching all age groups and to be changing the attitudes of the older age group.

The research has thus been effective in contributing to the change in the advertising which in turn has encouraged more people of all age groups to install smoke alarms and thus to save more lives than might otherwise have been the case.

8

TV-am

TARGET GROUP RATINGS

SUMMARY

The Business Background and Environment

The challenges facing TV airtime sales people, advertisers, agency planners and agency buyers in the short to medium term are immense. Dynamic changes in the structure of programme provision, resulting in consequent changes in viewing patterns, will lead to more fragmented audiences and intense competition for advertising revenue among media owners.

The need for a database which can cut through the vast amount of audience and market data available in the UK had become increasingly paramount. Such a database would provide TV sales people and their agency/advertiser counterparts with information that would facilitate effective targeting and minimise wastage in advertising monies.

The Development of the Research Database

BMRB developed a specialist research tool 'Target Group Ratings' (TGR) via the fusion of BARB data and TGI data. This was intended specifically to enable advertisers, agencies and TV contractors to buy and sell target audiences (comprising people who actually use a producer service) more accurately and cost effectively in the new era of fragmented audiences.

The development of the new fused TGR database was a major undertaking. During the 1980s BMRB closely monitored the developments in fusion work throughout Europe. This allowed BMRB to highlight the key issues for structuring our own fusion.

These key areas were: the identification of common variables, the importance weights that need to be attached to variables, the *direction* of the fusion, and the ratio of the sample size between donor and recipient. These issues were all, slowly and painstakingly, addressed through experimental work.

The result was the successful fusion of the latest six months of TGI respondents to the BARB sample. The *direction* of the fusion, from TGI to BARB, was critical as BARB data is sacrosanct and, to provide the most effective tool, it was necessary for all product usage and lifestyle data to be fused to the existing 'Gold Standard' TV data.

The fused database received BARB's seal of approval following an in-depth analysis of the fusion technique by an independent company Ken Baker Associates. In their conclusion they stated:

> "For a vast range of products for which advertising is extensively conducted, i.e. FMCG and consumer durables, we believe the BARB/TGI fusion is almost as accurate as it would have been if single source data had been collected."

The Value to the Client TV-am

BMRB launched the fused database 'Target Group Ratings' on April 10th 1990, the first TGI clients to be provided with Target Group Ratings were TV-am and Bartle Bogle Hegarty.

TV-am had already been extremely successful in generating advertising revenue with a viewer profile which is particularly attractive to advertisers aiming their commercial messages at the 'younger adult' demographic groups.

But TV-am's success in attracting these advertisers had led to the growth of a widely-held misconception that TV-am was a narrow medium, appealing only to this fairly tightly-targeted group of younger viewers. TV-am therefore had a major need to look at viewing profiles based on product usage rather than simple demographics if they were to make inroads into a wider market of advertisers. The company found exactly what it needed in the TGR research database.

This has proved highly successful for TV-am in its use in presentations to agencies and advertisers. For the first time, it has been possible to pinpoint the proportion of the viewing audience who actually use a product or service, and track this proportion at all viewing times across the day. This facility has proved most advantageous to TV-am in its efforts to show advertisers in certain market sectors (financial and motoring for example) that a higher proportion of TV-am viewers are highly active in their market than is the case among ITV viewers at other times of the day.

Target Group Ratings has now become a central tool in the marketing mix available to TV-am. In addition to playing a *dominant* part in the decisions of Citroën and Nationwide to use the breakfast-time station (resulting in revenues of close to one third of one million pounds for TV-am), TGR data is now included in all sales presentations. BMRB's fused database has played a significant role in maintaining TV-am's success in increasing the company's share of TV advertising revenue in times of economic recession.

For BMRB the research investment (which runs into six figures) has resulted in greater participation in the TV industry by offering a database that allows better targeting of television airtime. To date a total of eight advertising agencies and three television contractors are using Target Group Ratings data.

*   *   *   *   *

BUSINESS BACKGROUND AND ENVIRONMENT

British television is currently experiencing a period of dynamic change. The vastly increased choice of programming available to viewers able to receive satellite- and cable-delivered services (currently 2.0 million homes [1], and growing steadily) will, it is hoped, increase total viewing levels; but the inevitable fragmentation of viewing that will result from increased viewer choice will also make it more difficult for advertisers and their agencies to reach potential customers with their advertising messages. A national commercial Channel Five will further complicate matters within two or three years, providing added choice in 70% of UK homes.

These dynamic changes will accelerate the decline away from 'family unit' viewing; a decline that has been gathering pace throughout the 1980s with the advent of multi-set homes (currently 46% of all homes [2]), the growth of video cassette recorder usage (currently in 67% of all homes), and the launch of Channel 4, Breakfast television services and 24-hour programming. As a result of current and predicted changes in viewing patterns, the emergence of new sales organisations and new techniques in

(1) Source: New Media Markets, June 20 1991
(2) Source: AGB Trends in Television, May 1991

the sale and purchase of TV airtime have become necessary, as competition for advertising revenue becomes more intense. BMRB has developed a specialist research tool – Target Group Ratings (the fusion of BARB and TGI) – specifically to enable advertisers, agencies and TV contractors to buy and sell target audiences more accurately and cost-effectively in the new era of fragmented audiences.

THE HISTORICAL DEVELOPMENT OF TGI IN MEETING THE NEEDS OF THE MEDIA INDUSTRY

The TGI was launched by BMRB in 1968 as a 78 page self completion questionnaire that covered both product usership and media consumption (including TV viewing, readership and radio listening). In the early days of TGI the TV viewing data was collected in much the same way as readership (i.e. How many times did you view in the last month?) and the size of the questionnaire was predominantly restricted by the requirements of punch-coding.

Computer-aided document reading had been developed and was introduced in the fifth survey (1973). This resulted in a much slimmer (56 page) questionnaire. Since then the size of the questionnaire has continued to increase gradually, year by year, as clients have recognised the value of the TGI and requested more detailed information on growth markets.

Specially tailored analysis for individual clients (as opposed to generally available hardcopy books) became available in 1977 and, in 1984 BMRB introduced 'Lifestyle' statements onto the TGI in a controlled experiment. These became a permanent feature in 1986.

Today, the TGI is a self-completion survey placed at the end of BMRB's omnibus service, providing product and media information based on a sample of 25,000 adults per annum.

Purchase and media usage data are collected through the self-completion questionnaire and cover users of around 400 product fields and 3,500 brands. Within the field of press media planning and buying, TGI became established as a prime analysis tool and, indeed, achieved the status of a currency. In the area of television negotiation it has been, until now, of secondary importance despite the inclusion of regional TV data, a variety of TV questions covering availability to view and programmes that respondents 'specially choose to watch'.

The TGI is frequently referred to as 'The Planners Bible' and has been constantly revised and updated to ensure that it remains central to the users' requirements. From a base of predominantly press and television clients in 1970 (51 clients) the TGI is now utilised by over 200 different companies including all major media owners, nearly 80 advertising agencies and 50 advertisers.

THE DEVELOPMENT OF FUSION AS A RESEARCH TOOL

Throughout the 1980s it became clear that the problems surrounding single source data (i.e. high research costs, respondent overload, panel drop-out) would not be resolved in the foreseeable future. Attention turned to the idea of 'fusion', whereby two quite distinct research databases made up of different sorts of research covering mainly different questions could be merged together. There were a growing number of experiments being conducted in both the UK and elsewhere in Europe.

BMRB took a serious interest in the developments and, for the purpose of this paper, we have summarised the work and conclusions in chronological order below:

Timetable of Fusion Developments

1982

In France a self-administered questionnaire was placed with the second and third waves (a nationally representative sample of about 5,000 for each wave) of the CESP press and cinema audience survey. This data was then fused to the first wave file such that information on products and brands were injected for each respondent on the first wave. This was renewed and enlarged in 1984.

1984

The earlier 1982 survey was enlarged to cover the three waves of press and cinema plus three waves of radio and television audience surveys. People interviewed for the second wave of both surveys were asked to complete a self-administered questionnaire for 280 product fields and 3,000 products. The fusion used Gilles Santini's 'marriage' algorithm for technique. Its result was that complete information was available for *all* respondents, but the results did not provide the optimised environment to conduct valid tests.

1984-6

In Germany, Friedrich Wendt on behalf of the Media Analysis Association (AG.MA), developed the formation of a 'partnership model' built from the data acquired from separate samples using various measurement techniques. These comprised the broadcast media tranche (15,000 interviews) and print media section (18,000 interviews). The Technical Commission and the Working Party of AG.MA gave the fusion the 'green light', but highlighted problem areas covering the role, scope and weighting of common characteristics, the different degrees of representation with disproportionate samples and the smoothing effects.

1986

In Britain, FRS and IMS (UK) conducted the country's first ever fusion exercise in the media market by fusing the Financial Research Services (FRS) with the National Readership Survey (NRS). The technical consultant, James Rothman (*Admap* 1983), commented that:

> "The view we have formed from these tests is that, as it stands at present, the NRS/FRS data fusion is not sufficiently accurate. This is not too surprising considering it was the first attempt to fuse two very complex surveys. I do not think it is technically impossible to have an acceptable fusion between FRS and NRS... Fusion requires more computer power and more brain power than single source surveys but... there will be a saving on fieldwork costs."

1989

The Market Research Development Fund conducted a project to evaluate Santini's data-marriage technique using the TGI database. They found that simulated single source results from the fused database compared well with actual TGI results.

1989

Granada TV and RSMB fused respondents on BARB to Granada's omnibus survey 'G-Track'. The principle of this fusion was to identify the BARB panel member who was closest to a particular G-Track respondent in terms of their 'distance measurement'. In this instance the BARB respondent was 'donor' and G-Track respondent was 'recipient'. G-Track and BARB respondents were matched on a one-to-one basis for as many key demographics (common variables) as possible and *their viewing assumed to be the same*.

THE FUSION OF BARB AND TGI: THE TECHNICAL OBJECTIVES AND THE METHODOLOGY

This work, provided by RSMB and Granada provided the break-through for which BMRB was looking, so that it could fuse TGI to BARB. The objectives, if TGI was to provide a valuable research tool, were to be:

- the need to retain the existing 'currency' for planning and buying television ('BARB').
- the ability to target based on behavioural data rather than demographics.
- the fusion of TGI and BARB must be optimised to maintain an effective sample size.
- as many common variables as possible should be available.
- weight of viewing, for both commercial and total television, should be used as common variables.

In approaching the fusion of TGI and BARB, BMRB commissioned RSMB who had developed an algorithm based upon Mahalanobis' distance measurement. This technique had been utilised in the fusion of G-Track and BARB. We were able to call upon much of the experience of all these previous fusions and highlighted the key areas to which we must pay attention in structuring our own fusion. There were:

- the common variables.
- the importance weights.
- the direction of the fusion.
- the ratio of the sample size between donor and recipient.

These we will discuss further under the research methodology. A technical report on the TGI/BARB fusion was conducted in February/March 1990 on behalf of BARB by Ken Baker Associates. This covers the technical aspects, results and the phenomenon of regression to the mean in some detail, and is available from BMRB. Here we will outline the technique as simply as possible.

The aim of the fusion is to find the best match between the two sets of respondents being compared. The variables common to the full samples of potential 'donors' and 'recipients' are identified and then summed in order that the closest available individual donor for each individual recipient is selected. In order to maximise the use of the donor sample, and minimise the number of times a donor was selected twice, penalty weights were imposed on some donors, once they had been selected.

The distance measurement can be calculated in numerical terms by setting 'ranges' for each of the variables e.g:

Table 1   The Distance Measurement

	TGI Respondent	BARB Respondent	Distance Measurement
Age	27	27	0
Social Grade	C1	C1	0
Child Status	1	1	0
Working Status	Full	Full	0
Size of Household	4	2	0.5
etc.,			

In this example, for four common variables, the donor and recipient match exactly, the only difference occurs on size of household. This process would be *simultaneously* applied to all the common variables in order that the sum of distances between each donor and each recipient can be measured. If all the distance scores between a donor and recipient were zero, a perfect match would be achieved. However this is all but impossible and the final fusion solution involves a trade-off between the lowest possible distance measurement and the largest possible effective sample.

The quality of a data fusion relies heavily on the set of common variables that are available to form a link between donor and recipient. In addition to the eleven identical variables in both BARB and TGI we were able to create two more variables that, following the G-Track work, we felt to be important, namely total television and commercial television weight of viewing. All thirteen common variables are detailed in Appendix 1. However they were not all given the same weight.

For sex we felt it was essential that there was 100% matching, and so we deemed this to be a critical variable, with separate fusions conducted for males and females. For the rest we conducted substantial experimental analysis to establish the relative importance of each of the common variables. The statistical techniques are complex. Several techniques were tried and rejected including dummy multiple regression and canonical correlation. Eventually we used analysis of variance. The twelve common variables (within sex) were used in the analyses of variance to explain a selection of TGI and BARB data.

Some common variables were found to be important across most data items, some were rarely important and some were very important in certain areas.

The third area to be addressed was the direction in which the fusion was conducted. Our early experimental work had fused the TV viewing onto the TGI database (as had Granada's G-Track). However our objective was to add behavioural data as an enhanced targeting facility to BARB, therefore the BARB currency or 'gold standard' had to remain sacrosanct. A fusion, in the opposite direction, i.e. *from* TGI *to* BARB, would not alter this currency *and* it would provide significantly enhanced targeting opportunities. Thus the final solution was a fusion in this direction.

The final stage was to consider the ratio of donors to recipients. To do this we again fused the TGI with itself in order to simulate different ratios. We wanted to see whether we should fuse all of TGI to BARB (4:1), fuse six months field work only (2:1) or carry out a 1:1 fusion using a representative sub-sample of the database. In order to best assess this we had to look at both the effective sample each ratio would generate and the total distance measurement we would achieve in each different solution.

Analysis of the effective sample size using differing ratios of donors to recipients highlighted some interesting facts. The effective sample size was 85% on a 1:1 basis, which increased substantially to 98% on a 4:1 fusion with almost all donors only used once. A similar pattern emerged from the 2:1 fusion where a 99% effective sample was achieved.

In both the effective sample and the distance measurement the 2:1 fusion performed extremely well. This gave us the opportunity to use the more up to date six-monthly TGI data, and to perform two major fusions each year as the new TGI data became available. Using this methodology we needed to determine the best way to deal with the intervening months between major fusions, as although the BARB panel data is continuous it does suffer, like any panel, from drop-out and therefore some donors would have lost their recipient and likewise some new panel members would not have been attached to a donor. It was decided, therefore, that it would be necessary to repeat the fusion every quarter in order to keep the fused database reasonably current.

THE FUSED DATABASE EMERGES: THE BIRTH OF TGR

After all the areas we have discussed had been explored and the optimum solution for each issue achieved, we were finally in a position to conduct the fusion of the TGI onto BARB. Using our 2:1 solutions we took data from TGI for the six months ending April 1989 and fused this onto the BARB continuous panel for the four weeks ending 29th October 1989. The fusion was done independently for men and women and each ITV region was taken separately. In each case the actual fusion was extremely close to that achievable using the nearest neighbour solutions.

Having ascertained that the matchings we achieved on the TGI:BARB fusion were statistically valid we began to analyse some findings from the fused database. The initial results highlighted significant opportunities for buyers and sellers of TV data especially when targeting closely defined groups such as CD player owners. Table 2 highlights the difference in viewing levels of this particular group when comparing the strength of Friday evening versus the weakness of Saturday evening.

Table 2   CD player owners indexed on all adults w/e 3rd March

	Friday	Saturday
10:00pm	145	70
10:15pm	188	56
10:30pm	158	78
10:45pm	125	62

The problems faced by the fusion were two-fold. Firstly the nature of the BARB panel is that, as a *continuously* reporting panel, it will be prone to panel drop-out. As a result BMRB decided that a smaller quarterly fusion should be conducted for all new BARB respondents to ensure adequate regional sample sizes.

Secondly the planners, buyers and sellers required access to the fused (TGR) data on a daily basis. In answer to this problem BMRB sought agreements with DDS, AGB, RSMB and Media Audits to provide TGR data within the existing systems that they provided to the industry. In the final outcome only RSMB, AGB and Media Audits provided *access* to TGR data and no information was available on-line. This was to cause problems for TGR which we return to later.

BARB had shown a very keen interest in the developmental work at all stages of the project and appointed an independent consultant, Ken Baker Associates, to evaluate the fusion and produce a technical report. In his conclusion Ken Baker states:

> "For a vast range of products for which advertising is extensively conducted, i.e. FMCG and consumer durables, we believe the BARB/TGI fusion is almost as accurate as it would have been if single source data had been collected... The accuracy of the BARB/TGI fusion occurred as a result of scientific application of advanced statistical techniques to the problem to be solved."

BARB gave the fusion its full seal of approval and, on April 10th 1990, BMRB launched the fused database 'Target Group Ratings'. The first TGI clients to be provided with Target Group Ratings were TV-am, the breakfast-time ITV company, and advertising agency, Bartle Bogle Hegarty.

From the outset TV-am were very enthusiastic about this development and were confident that TGR's could provide added value to presentations across the complete range of product and lifestyle areas. Confident that a multi-channel future governed initially by steep economic recession would place more reliance on *targeting*, TV-am was quick to grasp the potential of a database that uniquely displays the proportion of the viewing audience at any time that actually uses a client's product or service. Before proceeding to a discussion of TV-am's use of the TGR database, we must look at the particular issues the company was facing.

THE BUSINESS ISSUES FACING TV-am

TV-am is the newest and most profitable station on the ITV network. Launched in February 1983 it is viewed by 7 million individuals each morning, rising to 16 million over the course of each week.

Viewing levels at breakfast-time are considerably lower than in the peak-time evening viewing period; nevertheless, TV-am has been extremely successful in attracting advertising revenue as a result of the development of a fast-moving programme format combining news, current affairs, human interest stories and celebrity guests, which has made the viewing profile of the station particularly attractive to advertisers aiming their commercial messages at the 'housewives with children', 'children', 'young adults' and (particularly) 'young women' demographic groups.

TV-am's success in attracting these advertisers has, however, led to the growth of a widely-held misconception that TV-am is a narrow medium appealing only to a tightly targeted group of viewers. In fact, TV-am's varied output allows for quite diverse targeting, and the different audience profile delivered to advertisers by the Channel Four Daily at breakfast-time (TV-am sells the airtime for this service) has, since April 1989, provided enhanced targeting opportunities.

TV-am is *not* a narrow medium; but it does have a considerably more youthful profile than does ITV at all other times of the day: hence the misconceptions of advertisers and agencies. Age profiles are compared in table 3:

Table 3   Audience Profile: TV-am vs ITV day-parts

	UK Population %	TV-am %	ITV 09:25-12:00 %	ITV 12:00-18:00 %	ITV 18:00-23:00 %
4-15 years	17	16	9	16	9
16-44 years	44	50	49	35	33
45 years	39	34	42	49	58

Base: Individuals aged 4+
Source: BARB,4 – w/e 17 March 1991

TV-am's weekday audience profile is, in fact, remarkably representative of the UK given the behavioural and attitudinal constraints inherent in the busy breakfast-time daypart, whereas ITV's audience is heavily biased towards older viewers. Nevertheless, the wrongly perceived idea of TV-am as a narrow, biased medium remains.

It is therefore vital that TV-am markets its airtime efficiently by highlighting the close fit between the purchase/usage profile of a client's product with the viewing profile of TV-am viewers. With the advent of increased competition in the commercial TV marketplace as described in the introduction above, the requirement for enhanced information on effective targeting in order to remain at the vanguard of effective TV sales has become imperative.

TV-am has historically invested substantially in commercially-available research databases and ad hoc research in order to present advertisers and agencies with details of the strengths of TV-am's audience profile vis-à-vis a range of products, goods and services.

However, the matching of a product to an audience has only allowed for comparisons to be made on industry-standard main- and sub-demographics, and even cross-tabulation special analysis on the basic TGI does not allow for the 'fusion' of viewing levels with purchasing behaviour.

This was always a problem for TV-am when attempting to entice high profile advertisers in the financial, motoring and corporate sectors on to their screens. TV-am's own qualitative research projects revealed very high activity rates in the financial and motoring sectors amongst young adults in general and young women in particular; and BARB data shows TV-am's audience contains a greater proportion of ABC1's than any ITV daypart pre-21:00 hours.

However, these advertisers and their agencies still had firm views on the type of advertiser that 'sits comfortably' in commercial breaks at breakfast-time, and TV-am found great difficulty in dynamically and substantially expanding its client base away from the FMCG/toys/leisure areas with which it had historically been associated.

TV-am was the first contractor to purchase TGR's and immediately set about making it work for them in their presentations. Initially, TGR information was included in traditional Housewives with Children and Young Housewife presentations to give added weight to research from other commercially available databases and to TV-am's own ad hoc research projects. However, analysis of some more unusual purchases/activities such as house purchases, bank and building society account holders for financial advertisers, and car ownership for motor manufacturers, created valuable ammunition for attracting advertisers who had, until now, remained difficult to convince of TV-am's unique advantages.

TV-am's USE OF THE RESEARCH

Some aspects of TV-am's use of TGR must remain confidential. However, two short case studies will give a flavour of the immense value the research database has been to the company.

Citroën Cars

During one of TV-am's presentations to the Mediastar media independent in November 1990, the question of why Citroën Car campaigns were not included in any TV-am schedules was raised. The reason given was that the client perceived TV-am as the wrong environment to warrant a share of the advertising budget. Nevertheless, the agency invited TV-am to present to them their ideas which would be passed on to Citroën UK.

Without doubt, this was a very difficult task since, at that time, the message of TV-am's relative upmarket profile was not commonly known and Citroën were adamant that they would only be buying ABC1 Adults.

A presentation was duly compiled and presented to Mediastar in December 1990. Its content highlighted TV-am/Channel 4 Daily's specific programmes, coverage of desired demographics, attention value statements and favourable TGI lifestyle statements. However, it was not until TGR information was added in the form of relating recent car purchases to audiences that a truly advantageous picture emerged.

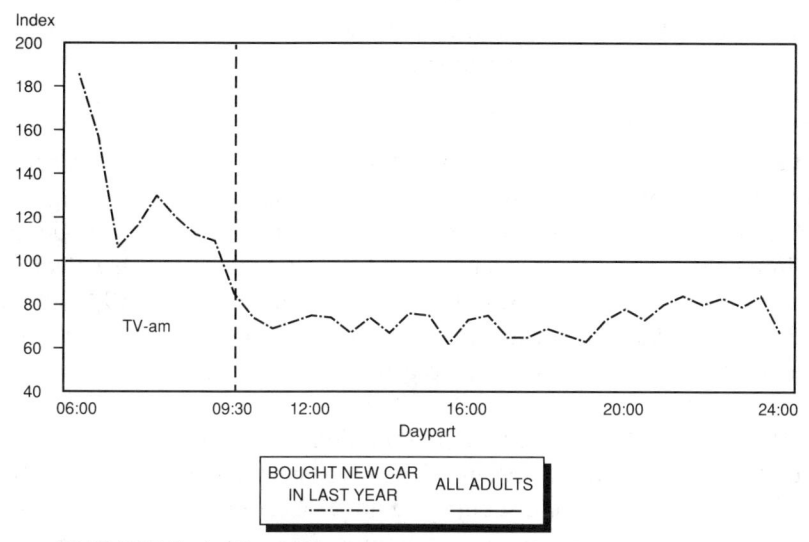

Figure 1   Bought new car in the last 12 months

Source: BARB/TGR Fusion Oct. 1990
Base: All adults.

TGR data was displayed graphically (Figure 1) by indexing purchaser ratings to all adult TV Ratings (TVRs) over a four week period. This clearly showed that TV-am's relatively youthful adult viewers had a higher propensity to purchase more new cars than those of any other ITV daypart; TV-am's average index was 130 versus 80 on ITV/C4.

Moreover, the real worth of TGRs to the Citroën presentation was that they indicated precisely the best times of the ITV day to reach prospective new car purchasers. This analysis was compared to where Citroën had traditionally placed its airtime. From such examination the early peak segment (17:30-20:00) which was Citroën's preferred daypart (accounting for 42% of commercial messages) was shown to be a poor time to reach the real target audience. These results, together with the TGRs for the TV-am segment, strengthened the TV-am argument. The fusing of TGI with BARB data assisted TV-am by:

- Confirming other TV-am research which indicated that their viewers were adventurous and desired the purchase of large items such as cars.

- Aided targeting within the TV-am daypart (06:00-07:00).

Citroën were impressed, and in January 1991 signed a deal for a sum in excess of £100,000 worth of advertising on TV-am which commenced in February. Prospects for future monies are excellent.

Nationwide Building Society

TV-am has, since its inception, attracted small amounts of financial advertisers' money, but frequently TV-am was seen as an afterthought and sales executives had to work hard to achieve minuscule shares of budgets.

In January 1991, Leagas Delaney told TV-am that they were welcome to make a pitch to Nationwide Building Society for a slice of their 1991 activity, although the likelihood of success was minimal. Above all, Leagas Delaney warned them that Nationwide were looking for more than a 'numbers' presentation.

The format of the eventual presentation had to reflect this. TV-am therefore expounded the virtues of the diverse composition of the TV-am audience with the aim of discouraging misconceived thoughts of the 'type' of advertiser TV-am can best accommodate. Again the presentation reviewed lifestyle statements, TV indices and especially commissioned qualitative research.

Nevertheless, there was no direct correlation between the holders of financial services and Nationwide customers and the relative viewing levels of the TV-am audience.

TGR provided the answer. Initially, TV-am used fused data (Figure 2) to highlight their viewers' preference for mortgage account ownership by indexing 'holders of mortgages' ratings on adult ITV/C4 viewership data.

This revealed that TV-am viewers had a greater propensity to hold a mortgage or joint mortgage policy than other ITV viewers. Moreover, the TV-am average index of 110 was higher than all other dayparts, including the late peak segment (95) which includes *News at Ten*, which is traditionally seen as the most appropriate time to reach financial decision makers.

Also the TGR graph (Figure 2) emphasised the most effective time to use TV-am – pre-07:30. This corresponded to other research TV-am had carried out which showed that early TV-am viewers (working adults) were particularly likely to hold a mortgage.

Figure 2   Targeting Mortgage Holders

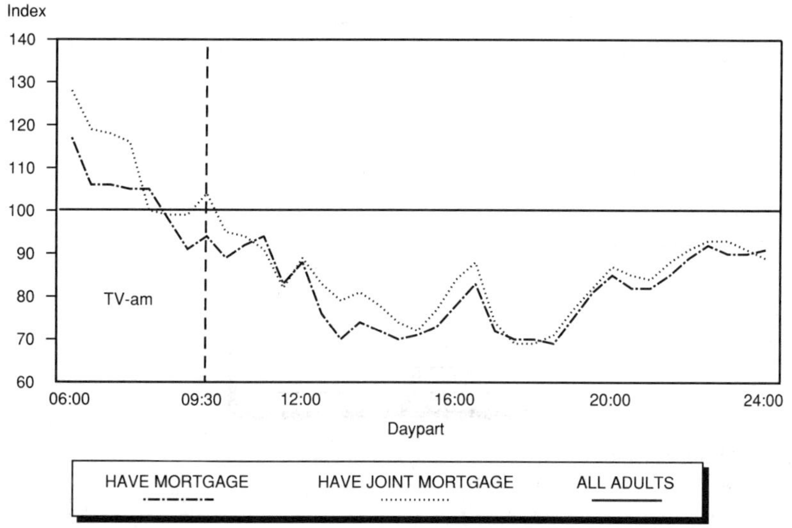

HAVE MORTGAGE   HAVE JOINT MORTGAGE   ALL ADULTS

Base: All adults (ITV)
Source: BARB/TGR Fusion Feb. 1991.

The TV-am argument was further strengthened by TGR data on Nationwide account holders. With the advent of branded information in January 1991 actual Nationwide account holder ratings were possible. Indexing Nationwide customers against all adults (Figure 3) the results here were similar to the analysis of all mortgage holders, i.e. the best indices were for TV-am pre 07:30 and the weakness of all other ITV dayparts were exposed.

However, the issue of TV-am's relative cost still had to be addressed. Again fused data had a major role to play. By revealing poor times of the

ITV day such as 12:00-18:00 for reaching prospective Nationwide customers, TV-am could measure its degree of cost advantage over such dayparts. Cost per thousand analysis proved TV-am's price competitiveness over ITV in the afternoon. Furthermore, by providing evidence that coverage would not suffer if TV-am were included in a schedule, the case for TV-am was complete.

Figure 3   Targeting Nationwide Account Holders

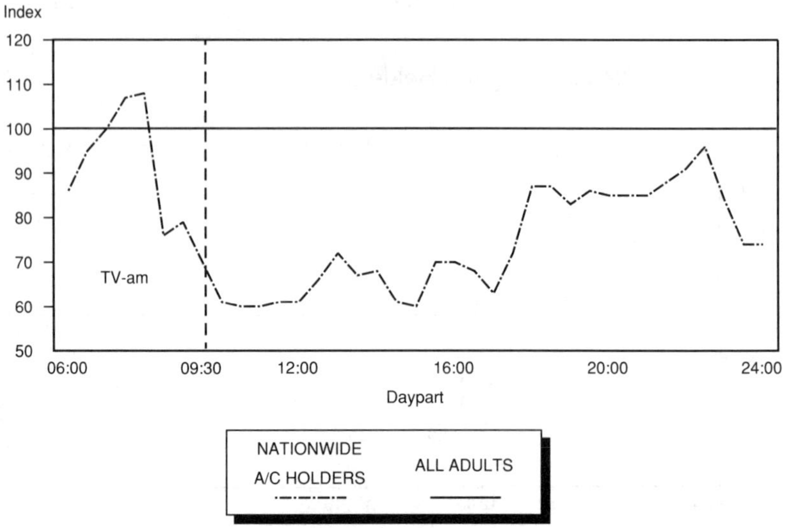

NATIONWIDE A/C HOLDERS
ALL ADULTS

Base: All adults (ITV)
Source: BARB/TGR Fusion Feb. 1991

As a result of the presentation, and the strength of the TGR data, Nationwide agreed to experiment with TV-am for the first time. A substantial six figure sum was committed with the promise of more in the future.

EFFECT ON TV-am's MARKET

For many years TV-am has communicated the view that its programme viewer profile is as diverse as any other ITV/C4 daypart. Moreover, its relatively youthful adult audience makes more major purchasing decisions than other older groups which therefore allows advertisers to target them through TV-am better than through other media.

Independent research has confirmed this, but the absence of industry accepted data has enabled sceptics to ignore this message.

The fusing of BARB ratings with TGI data has allowed TV-am in many instances to prove quantatively that its audience is:

- mobile.
- consumer oriented.
- aware of advertising.
- highly likely to try new products and brands.
- innovative.

Through the example of Citroën Cars and Nationwide, and other successful pitches which include TGR research, advertisers and agencies are now experimenting and using the targeting opportunities of TV-am.

TGR has now become a central tool in the marketing mix available to TV-am. In addition to playing a dominant part in the decisions of Citröen Cars and Nationwide Building Society to use TV-am, the use of TGR has played a significant role in maintaining TV-am's success in increasing the company's share of TV advertising revenue in times of economic recession.

For BMRB the research investment (which has run into six figures) has resulted in greater participation within the TV industry offering a research tool that can be used to aid the buying and selling of television airtime. To date a total of eight advertising agencies and three television contractors are using TGR data.

BMRB have further invested in PC software that allows clients to analyse BARB and TGR data in their own offices on their own PCs. This has been developed with input from a number of clients (including TV-am) and has provided the solution to one of the biggest problems – that of data delivery.

BMRB are about to conduct the next major fusion which will take place following the start of the new BARB system, in August 1991. This will provide further research problems, and marketing opportunities, as BARB will be implementing the Additional Panel Classifications plus a geodemographic segmentation (Pinpoint). Both of these enhancements will hopefully provide still more common variables with TGI and, enhance the quality of the new fusion still further.

APPENDICES

Appendix 1 – Common Variables

Sex	(2 Groups)
Age	(Actual)
Class	(5 Groups)
Household Status	(5 Groups)
Terminal Education Age	(4 Groups)
Household Size	(5 Groups)
Children 0-4	(Yes/No)
Children 5-15	(Yes/No)
Number of TV Sets	(3 Groups)
VCR Ownership	(Yes/No)
Working Status	(3 Groups)
Total Weight of Viewing	(5 Groups)
Commercial Weight of Viewing	(5 Groups)

Appendix 2 – References

Antoine, Jacques: "A case study illustrating the objectives and perspectives of fusion techniques"
3rd International Readership Symposium Salzburg (1985)

Antoine, Jacques & Santini, Gilles: "Fusion techniques : Alternative to Single-Source Methods"
European Research (1987)

Baker, Ken, Harris, Paul and O'Brien, John: "Data Fusion : An Appraisal and Experimental Evaluation"
MRS Conference, (1989)

Boucharenc, Lucien: "Rapprochement de donnees ou fusions d'enquetes"
IREP Seminar (1984)

Green, Andrew: "Media Research : What The Agencies Want"
Admap (1986)

O'Brien, Sarah & Wilcox, Steve: "The Marriage of BARB and G-Track : A Data Fusion Case Study"
Admap (1986)

Rothman, James:	"Data Fusion and Single Source Surveys" *Admap* (1988)
Rothman, James:	"Testing Data Fusion" ESOMAR (1988)
Ruhoman, Brian:	"Data Fusion : Its role in Media Research and Media Planning" *Admap* (1987)
Santini, Gilles:	"Fusion Processes : A conceptual and practical approach" SAMRA (1986)
Scheler, H & Wiegard, J:	"A report on experiments in fusion in the 'official' German media research (AG.MA)" 3rd International Symposium Salzburg (1986)
Wendt, Friedrich:	"The AG.MA model" Montreal Media Research Symposium (1983)

9

BARCLAYCARD

IT DOES MORE THAN YOU'D CREDIT

SUMMARY

The paper covers the research that was carried out on behalf of Barclaycard by Nielsen Consumer Research in January 1990, to identify the likely effect that the introduction of a fee would have on the Barclaycard customer base.

Barclaycard is the largest issuer of credit cards in the UK. Initially there were just two key players in the credit card market – Barclaycard and Access. However, in the early 1980s there was sustained growth in the credit card market and many other organisations issued credit cards. This led to greatly increased competition with the number of credit cards in issue increasing from 17 million in 1984 to almost 25 million in 1988.

Barclaycard's profitability was threatened. Barclaycard had made reasonable profits (£92m) in 1988, but was heading for diminished profit in 1989 and made a loss in 1990. Other factors were also contributing to this situation, and Barclaycard had to rethink its whole strategy. As a result two main marketing objectives evolved. These were firstly, to identify an alternative income stream and secondly, to develop a marketing policy so that its position as market leader could be maintained in the increasingly competitive financial services market.

A fee was seen to be the main alternative income stream and a number of factors were researched in terms of how it should be charged and at what level. An annual fee of £8 was used for the 1990 study.

As far as the relaunch of the brand was concerned, several different ideas were investigated with the over-riding objective being to minimise attrition so that the long term strategic advantage of a very large customer base could be maintained.

Nielsen Consumer Research was then commissioned to carry out a quantitative study to investigate four product options, the relative appeal of the new services and, most importantly, to determine which option gave Barclaycard the lowest attrition rate – the least number of cards returned.

In order to establish the likely attrition rate for the options, Barclaycard and Nielsen Consumer Research developed an attrition analysis based on inertia. This was to overcome the problem that people will claim to refuse to pay a fee, but in reality will accept it.

The preferred route was chosen not only because it met the two objectives, but the addition of MasterCard further helped to strengthen the offer.

In April 1990 Barclaycard announced the relaunch of its card with the reduction in the interest rate, the availability of MasterCard with the new services and the introduction of an annual fee.

Barclaycard was relieved that the prediction had been so accurate and that relatively few customers had been lost as a result of the introduction of the fee.

Barclaycard is again profitable as a result of these strategic changes which were strongly influenced by the outcome of the research conducted by Nielsen Consumer Research.

* * * * *

INTRODUCTION

This paper covers the research that was carried out, on behalf of Barclaycard by Nielsen Consumer Research, to identify the likely effect that the introduction of a fee would have on the Barclaycard customer base.

The research spanned nearly two years with a number of projects taking place during this time. This document will discuss these studies, but its main objective is to concentrate on the last piece of research that was conducted in January and February 1990 prior to the announcement of the fee in April 1990.

STRATEGIC BACKGROUND

Until recently the division of suppliers of credit card services in the UK had been according to membership of the two principal international payment systems – VISA and MasterCard. Barclaycard was the first company to launch a credit card in the UK and was a member of VISA. The other key player was Access, which was owned by a number of major banks and was a member of MasterCard/Eurocard.

In the early 1980s there was sustained growth in the credit card market and many other organisations started issuing credit cards. This led to greatly increased competition. Most of the newer entrants joined VISA, so that by March 1989 there were more than 30 issuers of VISA credit cards in the UK including several building societies. The number of credit cards in issue increased from 17 million in 1984 to almost 25 million in 1988. This growth is illustrated in Figure 1 below.

Figure 1   Number of credit cards issued (UK)

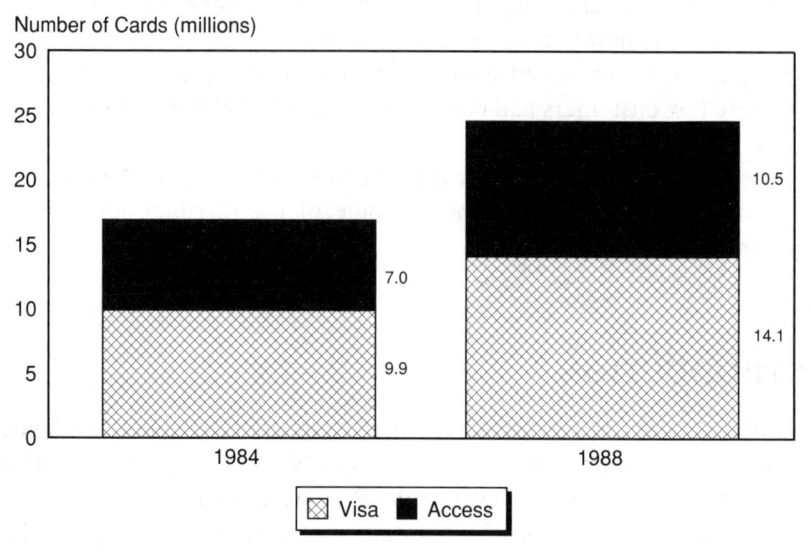

A further change taking place in the marketplace related to the processing of transactions. A number of banks applied for licenses to enable them to become members of both VISA and MasterCard/Eurocard. This meant that they could process both types of transaction and issue both types of card.

Profitability was threatened. Barclaycard had made reasonable profits (£92m) in 1988, but was heading for diminished profits in 1989 and made a loss in 1990.

Other factors were contributing to this situation. In addition to the growth in credit cards, debit cards were now becoming increasingly popular and were being offered by the banks and, in some cases, as an alternative to a credit card. Debit cards were also accepted by certain retailers who would not accept credit cards. Consequently the market was becoming even more divided.

Furthermore, the customers themselves were developing a more sophisticated approach in their use of credit cards. More people were tending to use their credit cards solely as a means of payment rather than credit and were clearing their monthly balance rather than paying interest on it.

Moreover, the merchant service charges from purchases made by credit cards was declining from approximately 3-4% to less than 2%.

The result of this was that Barclaycard had to re-think its whole strategy and as a result, two main marketing objectives evolved. These were firstly, to identify an alternative income stream and secondly, to develop a marketing policy so that its position as market leader could be maintained in the increasingly competitive financial services market.

As far as the other income streams were concerned, Barclaycard considered a number of options. A key area for improving income was seen to be in charging its customers a fee. There was certainly a culture developing whereby people had to pay for the financial services they received, but to what extent this was acceptable had not been fully investigated. Therefore questions like how to charge the fee, and how much the fee should be had to be answered. A number of research projects, both qualitative and quantitative, were carried out at this time to develop the idea of the fee. Barclaycard also spent a great deal of time investigating other countries' experiences. For example in America and, indeed many other European countries, it is the norm for fees to be charged for credit cards and for banking services.

Ideas for introducing the fee covered a transaction fee, a monthly fee and an annual fee. It was demonstrated that the first two were not suitable for a number of reasons. For example a monthly fee constantly reminds people that they are paying a fee and the wastage in administrative costs of sending out a monthly statement to people, who had not used their card that month, would be too high to make it a viable concern.

It was therefore considered that an annual fee should be charged. Research was then used to determine what level the fee should be and what effects the fee would have on the customer base. Qualitative and quantitative research was again carried out. It was demonstrated, particularly in the qualitative research, carried out by TQC, that consumers expectations were much higher than the levels Barclaycard was considering. The primary reason for this was that people's experience of charge cards was that of a fee in the region of £30 and not between £5-£15. Quantitative research carried out by Nielsen Consumer Research in 1988 and 1989 demonstrated that £8 would be the most preferable rate and this was, in fact, the fee level used for the 1990 study.

A major concern to Barclaycard was obviously how many customers they would lose if they did introduce a fee. In August 1988 and 1989 Nielsen Consumer Research investigated this. The findings of these two research projects suggested that the claimed level of returns could be as high as 60% of all cardholders at a fee level of £10. Even when accompanied by a reduction in interest rates the research results, at a superficial level, indicated that only 54% of customers would pay the fee.

The other factor that Barclaycard had to investigate if they were to introduce a fee, was when should they do it? Should they be the market pioneers or not? There were several advantages of being first in that it could be argued that it would mean the shedding of unprofitable customers, there would also be the P.R. benefits of being first; and being the first meant that they could set the tone and the price level. However, the disadvantage of being first was that Barclaycard could lose a substantial number of profitable customers because people would return their card and instead use a card that did not charge a fee, particularly if they already had more than one credit card. The argument in favour of being second was that people might believe that now that two companies had introduced a fee the rest would follow suit and therefore there would be little point in returning their card.

In the end, the decision of whether to be first or second was made for Barclaycard in that in August 1989 Lloyds Bank announced the introduction of a £12 fee on their Access card with their customers being mailed details of the fee in January 1990.

At the same time, Barclaycard were developing a marketing policy and were looking at ways to relaunch the brand with the fee being an integral part of this. Barclaycard had to be reasserted and made different from the other credit cards which were now becoming available. It basically needed more structure and a much clearer identity with added value services.

Consequently several different new products and services were devised, including:

Barclaycard International Rescue   Around the clock assistance for travellers.

Barclaycard Travel Accident Insurance	Automatic Travel accident insurance with cover worth up to £50,000.
Barclaycard Purchase Cover	Cover against theft, loss and accidental damage to anything paid for with a Barclaycard.
Barclaycard Connections	Assistance with household emergencies and expert advice on legal matters.

In addition, the idea of introducing the Barclaycard MasterCard at the same time as the new services, was suggested.

As well as doing this, the interest rate charged on outstanding balances was to be reduced from 29.8%, and the way in which the interest rate was calculated was to be changed. Furthermore, the idea of giving a guarantee of value to customers was put forward, i.e. people had the opportunity to claim back their fee if they cancelled the card.

By the end of 1989 Barclaycard had arrived at the stage whereby they had a new brand to launch which offered new services and had an annual fee. However, they had to be certain that this new brand met certain objectives which were to:

- minimise attrition, so that the long-term strategic advantage of a very large customer base would be maintained.

- obtain an acceptable rate of return for the product.

- make sure that the offer to cardholders would be seen by them and the media as a fair one in the circumstances.

- ensure the package supporting the development of the Barclaycard brand was 'superior', to increase its value and position it well for the longer term.

- make certain that no long-term damage was done to the product by the tactics of implementing the charges.

- confirm that the product was properly structured to allow long-term profitable growth under a wide range of assumptions about external variables.

In fact there was such concern over the likely loss of customers that it was felt necessary to have an alternative to this new brand. Consequently, two other options were put forward. One was the idea of not charging a fee, but increasing the interest rate. The other was to introduce a new card branded Barclays rather than Barclaycard. This would have no fee and no new services.

After in-depth consultation and research, four product options were finally developed. These were:

Option A: An annual fee would be introduced and the annual interest rate reduced to 25.3%. The new services would also be available. In addition, this option would give people the opportunity to apply for a Barclaycard MasterCard.

Option B: An annual fee would be introduced and the annual interest rate reduced to 25.3%. The new services would also be available.

Option C: This option would give people the choice of not paying a fee, but a higher rate of interest of 31.4% per annum would be charged instead. The new services would also be available.

Option D: A Barclaycard Card, which could be used in any VISA outlet. It would be provided free of charge, but with an annual interest rate of 29.9%. Holders of this card would not be eligible for the new services and the card would also have a shorter interest free period than Barclaycard.

Interestingly, Barclaycard's preferred option prior to the 1990 research was Option B, as it was seen to satisfy the two main marketing objectives in that it was relaunching the brand as well as providing another source of income.

Introducing a MasterCard at the same time was not favoured for a number of reasons. These included the fact that, in qualitative research projects, there was no real indication of any benefits of doing this. Furthermore, the enormous administrative problems that were likely to ensue in terms of coping with the introduction of a new card at the same time as handling all the likely cancelled cards, was somewhat daunting. In many ways, MasterCard was seen to have a life of its own and it was felt that it should be introduced either before the introduction of the fee or left until afterwards.

Therefore, combining the MasterCard with the relaunch of the Barclaycard brand was seen to be of secondary interest.

By this stage Barclaycard was in a position to research the product options in detail. Qualitative research was carried out and, at the same time, Nielsen Consumer Research was commissioned to undertake quantitative research to examine the response to the four main product options and to establish what effect each one would have on Barclaycard's customer base.

The principal objective of the quantitative research, conducted in January 1990 by Nielsen Consumer Research, was therefore to investigate which route gave Barclaycard the lowest attrition rate, i.e. the least number of cards returned.

From this, other objectives evolved, which were:

- to determine how many cardholders would pay an annual fee for an enhanced product.
- to look at the relative appeal of the various enhancements.
- to examine the potential switching to other brands of cards.
- to measure the choice between the enhanced fee bearing Barclaycard, and the free card options.
- to describe the types of Barclaycard holders who would either switch to a free card or relinquish their Barclaycard.

FORMULATION OF THE RESEARCH

When deciding what approach should be developed for the research, one major factor had to be borne in mind. This was that once Barclaycard introduced the fee there was no turning back. Therefore, the decision that they would reach regarding which option they should choose had to be the right one – there was no second chance.

As already mentioned, previous research suggested that the effects of introducing a fee could be catastrophic. Certainly the qualitative research demonstrated that people's immediate reaction to a fee was that it was a totally unacceptable proposal.

This study therefore had to demonstrate that the option that would finally be recommended had to have the most beneficial effect on Barclaycard's customer base.

It was therefore decided that the research should be made as realistic as possible. To this end, the options were developed into finished pack format with a brochure, letter and even new terms and conditions were provided for each one. The final packs used for the research were of excellent quality. It was a simulation exercise in that the letter was addressed to a 'real' person and not Mr A. N. Other and the suggested timing of the introduction of the fee was put as the following month rather than some vague time in the future. Some of the letters were in fact provided in different styles and they had to comply with all the legal requirements.

In addition to these 'macro' factors, several research orientated considerations had to be taken into account when formulating the research. These included:

1) the emotive nature of the subject matter

2) the sample size and structure

3) the length of the interview

4) the fact that various documentation had to be looked at by the respondents.

Consequently, it was felt that street, telephone and self-completion interviews were inappropriate due to the scope and type of information required. The only interviewing technique that could be used effectively was an in-home interview.

It was also essential that the research be carried out in utmost secrecy. Security was of great concern to Barclaycard and therefore the brochure packs had to be handled very carefully.

THE SAMPLE

As far as the sample was concerned, several conditions had to be adhered to.

Following on from previous research, Barclaycard wanted to interview just active users of Barclaycard (those people who have used a Barclaycard within the past six months to purchase something as opposed to using it as a cheque guarantee card). These people were to also represent the profile of Barclaycard holders in terms of age, sex, social class and regionality.

In addition, the sample had to reflect people's cardholding behaviour. Barclaycard required the correct proportions of multiple cardholders (those people who have another bank or building society credit or charge card) and solus cardholders. In addition, the sample was to be equally divided between payers (those who always pay off their bill) and borrowers (those who do not).

In order to satisfy the need to make the research as real as possible, each option had to be treated as a separate exercise. Consequently the sample structure for each was to be the same and was to take into account all the requirements outlined above. Furthermore, it had to be remembered that at the analysis stage, the groups were to be weighted to their correct proportions within the total level of Barclaycard cardholders.

In order to accommodate all these conditions in terms of structure and making the research as realistic as possible, it was deemed necessary to have a total sample size of 2,000 with 500 for each of the options.

None of the respondents was pre-recruited from lists. The Nielsen Consumer Research fieldforce interviewed the 2,000 respondents between 17th January and 13th February 1990 with the average length of the interview being 30 minutes.

ANALYSIS

Before the research was initiated, it was unclear as to what type of analysis would give Barclaycard the right answer with regard to the effect that the relaunch of the brand and the introduction of the fee would have. It was therefore decided that the actual research should be as straightforward as possible, but that it would use three different approaches. These were:

- the response to the brochure this would determine how the relaunch should be presented.

- a trade-off analysis this would assess the relative benefits of the new card.

- attrition analysis this would establish the effect the relaunch would have on the customer base.

To this end, the questionnaire was structured to incorporate these three areas, but it also included people's usage of credit cards, their banking, income and demographic details.

As the main aim of the research project was to look at the repercussions the relaunch might have on the customer base, the analysis that will be discussed in detail in this paper will be the attrition analysis.

However, it is important to realise that the trade-off analysis also played an important role not only for the reasons above, but also because it was used to develop the attrition analysis.

In addition, the response to the pack was of considerable interest because, if it had been negative, then the number of people planning to cancel their Barclaycard could have been very high. The packs had to be right and had to be presented as attractively and clearly as possible.

As far as the attrition analysis was concerned, the one that was finally developed took into account people's initial reactions to the fee, the effects of the trade-off and the inertia factor.

Using the trade-off as part of the attrition analysis was based on the premise that the more people talk about an idea the more likely they are to change from having a negative opinion to having a more positive one. It was felt that having spent a substantial proportion of the interview discussing the details of the credit card, both generally and in the trade-off, respondents thoughts would be focused on what they really wanted from a credit card, they would become less hostile to the idea of a fee and more ready to accept the view that they had to pay something for the new services offered by the revamped credit card.

The inertia factor was something that Barclaycard had been aware of, but had not really investigated fully and it had never been developed for a quantitative research project. The premise for the inertia factor was that initially people will claim that they will refuse to pay a fee and will return their card. However, in reality the results were likely to be less severe. Three factors contributed to this which were that:

a) the benefits of the new Barclaycard could be seen to outweigh the costs of paying the fee, so it could be argued that people would lose out if they did return their card.

b) people would believe that the effort of cancelling the card and applying for another one, because of the £8 fee, would not really be justifiable.

c) if one credit card company were introducing a fee, then others could follow so people would eventually pay a fee even if not with Barclaycard. This was particularly relevant when Lloyds had already announced their fee.

The attrition analysis was developed from the findings of the research using four key stages of the questionnaire to establish the true attrition rate. The structure of the analysis is outlined in Figure 2 below.

Figure 2   Attrition Analysis

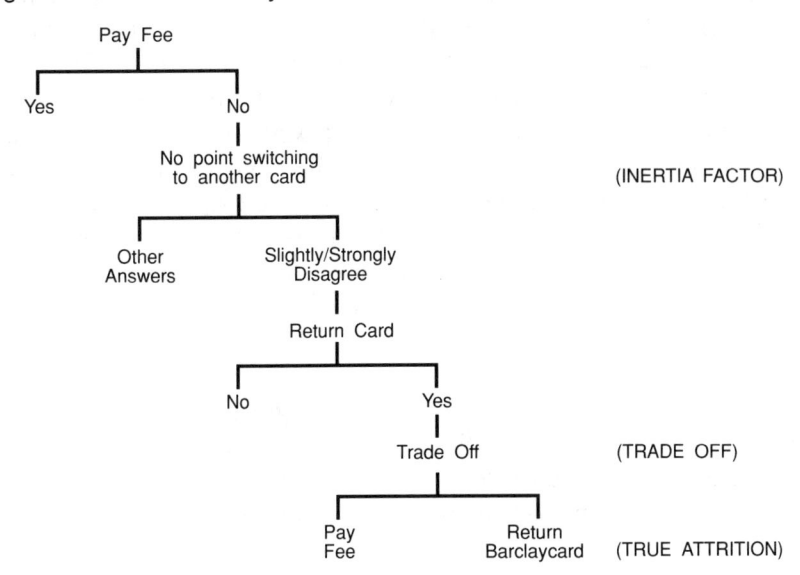

```
                    Pay Fee
                   ┌───┴───┐
                  Yes      No
                           │
                    No point switching
                     to another card                    (INERTIA FACTOR)
                   ┌───────┴───────┐
                 Other         Slightly/Strongly
                Answers           Disagree
                                     │
                                 Return Card
                               ┌─────┴─────┐
                              No           Yes
                                            │
                                        Trade Off       (TRADE OFF)
                                      ┌─────┴─────┐
                                     Pay        Return
                                     Fee       Barclaycard   (TRUE ATTRITION)
```

Base: All respondents

The analysis was carried out for each of the four options in order to assess which option had the highest level of attrition. For each one, not only was the total sample looked at, but also certain key variables namely, multicard versus solus cardholders and also payers versus borrowers (see section headed *The Sample* for definitions).

The reason for this, in the case of the multicard holders, was that they could just cancel their Barclaycard and use their other card. This would apply even if their other card was a Lloyds Access, the argument being that they would be prepared to pay one fee, but not two and with Lloyds already having charged the fee, Barclaycard would lose out.

As far as the borrowers were concerned it was imperative that they be retained as they contribute significantly to Barclaycard's profits. It was therefore essential to establish their likely attrition level, particularly in the case of Option C, where the interest rate was to be increased.

For the payers, although it could be argued that they were unprofitable, they still played an important part in the business in as much as they accounted for high levels of turnover and also income derived from the merchant service charge. They basically had to be maintained if economies of scale were to be achieved.

Not only was this analysis used to determine how many cards would be returned, but it also looked at the likely levels of new card applications. These included the relaunched Barclaycard itself, the take up of the MasterCard (from Option A) and the Barclaycard Card (Option D). It was necessary to do this because in any normal year a million new cards would be handled, apart from normal replacement of expired cards. Initial estimates had suggested that 1 million MasterCards alone could be applied for and the implications of coping with another year's processing squeezed into a month could be disastrous. Therefore it was felt that an awareness and inertia factor should be taken into account, in order to make these estimates more realistic.

RESULTS

As the results of the survey are highly confidential it is only possible to provide just the key findings. Nevertheless, the findings from the overall study were very acceptable in terms of people's attitudes to the four options, their response to the main changes being introduced, the different elements of the packs, etc.

As far as the attrition analysis was concerned the levels of attrition for each option are shown in Table 1 below.

Table 1

	Options			
	A	B	C	D
Initial Assessment/Reaction				
% of candidates saying they will return their card (%)	30	34	12	25
Final Assessment/Reaction*				
Prediction of number of cards likely to be returned ('000s)	571	640	131	384

Note: *Taking into account the trade-off analysis, inertia factor, etc.

In addition, the analysis also suggested that, in the case of Option A, 432,000 active account holders would apply for a MasterCard.

The trade-off analysis was able to provide the perceived monetary value for each of the new services.

CONCLUSIONS

The conclusion arrived at by Barclaycard on the basis of this research was that Option A, i.e. the introduction of the £8 fee, reduction of the interest rate, availability of the new services and the opportunity to apply for a MasterCard, was the one that should be introduced.

The reason for this was that, although the attrition levels were not as low as they were for Options C and D, it was widely accepted within Barclaycard that, long term, C and D were not viable options.

Option D, in Barclaycard's view, was never really a true option as it degraded both the product and Barclaycard's role in the marketplace as being *the* credit card company. D was only offered as an option because of Barclaycard's concern regarding the potential number of people cancelling their card and the effect that the fee might have on Barclaycard customer base.

Option C was not really going to be able to arrest the decline in profits because increasing the interest rate only affected the borrowers and, as they were a declining proportion of the customer base, it was likely that the effects would eventually be negligible. Therefore, the marketing objective of increasing income would not be met by this option.

Option B, as mentioned in the introduction, was the one that Barclaycard was originally keen to introduce. Certainly the attrition levels were still relatively high compared with C and D, but the actual costs to Barclaycard in terms of introducing the new services and reducing the interest rate were much lower. It was also predicted that long-term profitability would benefit from this option. Moreover, Option B met both of the main marketing objectives.

However, it was realised that having conducted the 1990 research an even better route should be considered, and that was Option A. All the factors influencing the choice of Option B still held true, but the addition of MasterCard further helped to 'soften the blow' of the fee. People's response to this was extremely positive and far higher than Barclaycard had anticipated prior to the research.

RECOMMENDATION

As a result of the research, it was therefore recommended that Barclaycard use Option A as a means of introducing the £8 fee. Certain provisos were included in the recommendation. For example, applications for the

MasterCard should be as straightforward as possible. The reason for this was that, if people already had a Barclaycard and had therefore been vetted, it would not be necessary to ask them to fill in another detailed form – a signature saying that they requested the card would suffice.

In order to control the effects of the likely take up of new MasterCards, it was suggested that only a selection of customers be mailed and that this be followed up in gradual stages to eventually include all active account holders.

Another recommendation was that the new services should be limited to the Barclaycard International Rescue, Travel Accident Insurance and Purchase Cover. The research had indicated that the others were not seen to be necessary and would only incur extra costs and administration problems.

ACTION TAKEN BY BARCLAYCARD

In May 1990 Barclaycard wrote to all its active account holders announcing the introduction of the fee (to be included in their June statements) together with a reduction in the interest rate, the availability of MasterCard and the new services.

This was done in exactly the same way as had been developed in the research in that a brochure, together with a letter giving details of the changes, was issued.

Preparation also had to be made for the large number of enquiries that would result from the introduction of a fee. In a normal month staff dealing with customers may handle up to 500,000 enquiries by telephone and post. These were expected to double in the peak months following the announcement. An extra 120 man years work had to be squeezed into a short period of time. Additional staff recruitment and training therefore had to be conducted. Seven million mail packs and items of stationery had to be prepared, and all routine work had to proceed as normal.

The organisation was bracing itself for a massive surge in enquiries. However, in the event the peaks were not quite as severe as anticipated and the administration was able to deal with all the enquiries without any real problems.

RESULTS OF THE BARCLAYCARD RELAUNCH

Barclaycard maintained a very close check on the card returns with up-dates being prepared daily. This included further research using the same methodology amongst cardholders, which was carried out continuously from the announcement of the changes in April 1990 through to September 1990.

By December 1990 the number of closures amongst active cardholders was 485,000. Referring back to the attrition analysis, at 95% confidence levels the forecast of 571,000 was plus or minus 140,000 accounts in statistical terms. This meant that the active attrition could have been as high as 710,000 and still have been within statistical limits. Yet, as has been shown, the actual level of returns was much closer to the one predicted.

As far as the take-up of MasterCards was concerned, by the end of 1990 it was about 664,000. Although this was somewhat higher than the 432,000 forecast, it must be remembered that the original forecast of card applications was 1 million which was then diluted to 432,000 by the attrition analysis.

CONCLUSIONS REACHED BY BARCLAYCARD

In general, Barclaycard was relieved that the prediction had been so accurate and that relatively few customers had been lost as a result of the introduction of the fee. Furthermore, the additional income that has been derived from the fee has made Barclaycard a profitable concern once more.

The relaunch of the brand culminating in the availability of the new services and of MasterCard has been demonstrated to have added to the brand profile and with its changed advertising strategy Barclaycard has now increased its market position.

Therefore, the research carried out, primarily by Nielsen Consumer Research, helped to ensure that the two marketing objectives initially set out by Barclaycard, i.e. to identify an alternative income stream and to develop a new marketing policy in order to maintain its position as market leader, were achieved.

154   Research Works

APPENDIX

Further developments have taken place since the introduction of the fee. Barclaycard has embarked on a new phase of advertising development to communicate the benefits of having a Barclaycard. This resulted in a memorable and enjoyable campaign featuring Rowan Atkinson in London...

...and in Moscow

Index

AA (Automobile Association) 41
AB TGI 64, 70, 72, 73, 74, 77, 79
Access 138, 140, 142
  Lloyds 149
Action Plan, Warwick District Council 48, 58, 61, 62
ADAS (Agricultural Development & Advisory Service) 86
Admap 123, 136, 137
Advisory Services to Agriculture report 87
AG.MA (Media Analysis Association) 123, 137
  partnership' model 123
  Technical Commission 123
  Working Party 123
AGB 109, 127
  Home Audit 105, 107, 116
Age Concern 3, 15
Alliance International Ltd 65, 72, 85
AMSO Award scheme 96
Annual Classic Car Show 35
Apricot Computers 65, 72
Audience Selection Ltd 2, 6, 7
  phonebus 7

BARB 63, 66, 69, 71, 118, 119, 121, 123, 124, 125, 126, 127, 128, 130, 132, 135, 136
Barclaycard 138
Bartle Bogle Hegarty 119, 128
BBC Radio 76
  Local 75
  National 75
BBC1 67, 68, 75
BBC2 67, 75
Bella 16
Best 16
Bill, The 69
BJM Research & Consultancy Ltd 92, 98, 99, 100, 102, 105, 107, 109
BMRB 64, 65, 66, 67, 70, 72, 74, 118, 119, 120, 121, 122, 127, 128, 135
  TMRB 74

BMRC 66, 78
BP (British Petroleum) 14
British Telecom 16
Bucket campaign, Home Office 105
BUPA 15
Business Development, Thames Television 63, 66

Capital City 69
Capital Radio
  FM 64, 68, 75
  Gold 68
Car a Day, Heinz 34, 38, 39, 41, 42
  1986 41
  1987 41
  1988 41
CATI (Computer Assisted Telephone Interviewing) 30, 74, 92
CESP 122
Channel 4 67, 75, 77, 120, 131, 134
Channel 4 Daily 129, 131
Channel Five 120
Charities Aid Foundation 5
Chat 16
Childline 16
Choice 15
CHOICES, Thames Television 65, 77, 78
Citizens' Charter 23, 25
Citroën Cars 120, 130, 132, 135
City Programme, The 68
Clarke Hooper 35, 38, 39, 40, 41
COI (Central Office of Information) 102
Compaq Computers 71
Consumers' Association 26
Coronation Street 68
Council for the Protection of Rural England 89
Council of Sales Promotions Agencies 42
Countryside Commission 89

Daily Mail 67
Daily Telegraph 67
DDS 127

155

Index

Districts, Royal Mail 24, 26, 27, 28, 29, 31
Doll's House campaign, Home Office 102, 103, 104, 105, 106, 107, 109, 113, 115, 116, 117
Driveaway, Heinz 34, 35, 39, 41
DTI (Department of Trade and Industry) 26, 27, 31
DVLA Select Registration 35, 41
Dying campaign, Home Office 103

End-to-End survey, Royal Mail 23, 24, 27, 29, 31, 32
Ernst and Young 30
Eurocard 140
Evening Standard 67

FCO 104, 115
Financial Times 64, 67
FMCG 119, 128, 130
FRS (Financial Research Services) 123
Fundraising and Publicity Conference, Samaritans 12
Fusion, TV-am 118, 122, 123, 124, 126, 127, 130, 135, 136, 137
FWAG (Farming and Wildlife Advisory Group) 95

G-Track, TV-am 123, 124, 125, 126, 136
Granada TV 123, 124
Guiding 15

Heinz 33
Home Office 102

IMS (UK) 123
Independent, The 67
Institute of Sales Promotions 42
ITCA 22
ITV 66, 68, 69, 75, 120, 129, 130, 131, 133, 134
  London 64, 72, 73, 74
  Thames 64, 67

Jazz FM 75
Just 17 15

Ken Baker Associates 119, 124, 128
Kish selection grid 21

LA Law 69
LBC Radio 64, 75
  Crown 75
  FM 68
  Talkback 68
Leagas Delaney 132
Living 16
Lloyds Bank 142, 148
London Fire and Civil Defence Association 107
London Match, The 69
LWT (London Weekend Television) 64, 67, 70, 77

MAFF (Ministry of Agriculture, Fisheries and Food) 86, 88, 89, 96
Management Retirement Guide 15
Market Research Development Fund 123
MasterCard 139, 140, 143, 144, 145, 150, 151, 152, 153
Match, The 69
Me 16
Media Audits 127
Media Campaign Services 85
Mediastar 130
Melody Radio 75
Midweek Sports Special 68
Mobile Befriending Centre, Samaritans 16
MORI (Market & Opinion Research International) 47, 48, 50, 51, 52, 56, 59, 62

NAO (National Audit Office) 86
National Children's Home 16
National Fundraising Day, Samaritans 12
National Rivers Authority 95
Nationwide Building Society 120, 132, 133, 135
NCC (National Consumer Council) 50
NCC (Nature Conservancy Council) 95
News at Ten 68, 69, 133
Next Steps, ADAS 89
Nicholson, Sir Bryan 30

Nielsen Consumer Research 138, 139, 142, 145, 147, 153
Nightline 16

Nine O'Clock News 68
NOP Market Research Ltd 2, 6, 7, 20
NRS (National Readership Survey) 123
NSPCC 3, 16

OMNIMAS 40
Outreach, Samaritans 3, 12, 14, 16, 18
  Elderly 14
  Events 15, 16
  Hospital 15
  Prison 16
  Rural 15, 16

Phonebus 7
Post Office 27, 30
POUNC (Post Office Users' National Council) 26, 27, 31
Promotion Unit, Samaritans 16
Public Accounts Committee, House of Commons 86, 88
Public Record, Royal Mail 24, 27

Quality of Service, Royal Mail 23, 24, 25, 26, 27, 29, 31, 32

Red Cross 15
Research International Ltd 23
Rothman, James 123
Rover 35, 39, 41
Royal Mail 23
RSMB 123, 127

Saatchi & Saatchi Advertising Ltd 2
Saga 15
Saira campaign 15, 19
Samaritan Week 13
Samaritans, The 1
Santini G. 'marriage algorithm' 122, 123
SMD (Standard Man Days), ADAS 97, 98, 99
South Bank Show, The 69
State Veterinary Service 88
Sun, The 16

Telethon 15
Tenant Satisfaction Survey, Warwick District Council 47
Tenants' Choice, Warwick District Council 48, 56, 57, 59

TGI 118, 119, 121, 122, 123, 124, 125, 126, 127, 128, 130, 131, 132, 135
TGR (Target Group Ratings) 118, 119, 120, 121, 128, 130, 131, 132, 134, 135
Thames Television 63
Times, The 64, 67
TN (Taylor Nelson) 33, 34, 37, 44
  PROFILE 38, 44
Total Quality Management, Royal Mail 24, 32
TQC 141
TUC 16
TV-am 118
TVR (TV Ratings) 131

Upbeat 15

VISA 140, 144

Walden, Brian 69
Warwick District Council 47
Wendt, Friedrich 123
WI (Women's Instiute) 15
Write Your Own Cheque, Heinz 34, 39, 40, 41, 42
WRVS 15

YMCA 16
Youth Club Federation 16